"Miracles and the Healing Power"

by

TODD DIXON, M.D.

DIXON PUBLISHING COMPANY

Dedicated to --

> *Gloria (my wife),*
>> *Michelle (my daughter),*
>>> *Sean (my son),*
> *and to God.*

SPECIAL THANKS

I want to thank all the people in this book, who shared their stories of being healed that others may benefit.

I want to thank my wife, Jerry Dixon, Betsy Coffman and Virginia Buchanan for their help in editing this book. I want to thank Mike Dixon for his advice.

Most of all I want to thank Terry. This gifted, beautiful being has opened my eyes to a dimension of reality I could not see. A reality where God, miracles and healing occur. She has helped me to experience a force that we all may tap into to heal ourselves. She is a pioneer, a healer and a friend, who gave me and my wife a miracle.

This book is about Terry, her healings, and the unlimited possibilities for all of us as we explore THE HEALING POWER.

*May God grant me the ability to write the truth
and my readers the ability to hear the truth.*

Miracles
and the
Healing
Power

〜〜〜〜〜〜〜〜〜〜〜〜〜〜〜〜〜

FOREWORD

I am devoutly Christian, and this source has been my strength and guidance in writing this book. The woman performing miracles, whom I'm writing about, also believes in Christ; however, she is able to see the divinity in all mankind and all religions.

TABLE OF CONTENTS

INTRODUCTION

Western medicine and technology are the best in the world, and the United States is the forerunner. With the invention of vaccines, the scourges such as polio and diphtheria are rarely seen. Antibiotics now kill the organisms that used to kill us. Liver and heart-lung transplants are becoming more and more frequent. The CAT scan and MRI (magnetic resonance imaging) give us amazingly clear pictures of the inside of our bodies. Knowledge of nutrition and exercise helps us live healthier life styles. Surgeons now perform surgery on fetuses inside the mother's womb and premature babies that weigh 1 pound 1 ounce are now being saved.

If we have the best medical technology in the world, why are so many people in the United States still very sick? Why do some people who are treated with drugs remain sick and others who are not get well? Is there

I

another factor at work here? This book is intended to shed light on this missing component in the healing process, an invisible and as yet unexplainable force which I will refer to as the healing power. The healing power shall be defined as "a universal force which creates positive changes in humans toward a state of health and well-being. Its purpose is life."

Medical doctors in the United States have been saturated with science. Understandably so, for science is based upon truth and has given us drugs and medical therapy which really work. Yet, the healing power is not discussed in medical school. Why? Because science has not adequately researched this most important area. One of the most famous quotes in medicine, by Ambroise Pareu in the sixteenth century, is "The surgeon dresses the wound and God heals the wound." Yet most doctors do not understand all the implications of this statement.

Scientists are on the way to proving the benefits of positive thinking and attitude. They are finding that a healthy mind can help heal a sick body. The current terminology used to describe the mind's ability to heal the body is called the mind-body connection. However, what is being overlooked is how the healing power is the catalyst for the mind-body connection.

It took personal misfortune to open my eyes to a force that can't be measured or seen, except through results. My wife and I were unable to conceive a child, although we used everything western medicine had to offer. With all medical alternatives exhausted, I turned at last to the healing power. Until I felt and EXPERIENCED the invisible force, I did not truly understand it. Now I can never forget it. I now know the vast, almost unlimited resource of power we may draw upon to improve our physical, mental and spiritual health. I now have a daughter and a son who are daily reminders to me of the most powerful combination of western medicine and the healing power.

Western medicine was built on science. A few of the cornerstones of science are open mindedness, the pursuit of truth and the saying "prove it." The skepticism which goes with this saying is good and necessary. It is only natural that before the medical and scientific communities will accept the healing power they will need scientific evidence. Very well, I will present evidence that this force exists.

The first step that I have taken is to provide case studies. I have researched 14 different cases of people who have been healed physically, mentally and spiritually by one extraordinary woman who has been given the gift of healing. As a doctor, I have examined the medical records before and after the healings to verify them. This book is being written from the medical and scientific perspective, because I feel this healing force can help millions of people and the medical community should be made aware of it. It is my firm belief that the most powerful tool to cure disease is modern day medical technology combined with the healing power. I believe this invisible force can be harnessed for the benefit of all mankind. I believe it is time.

CHAPTER ONE
TERRY'S STORY
(A Healer's Perspective)

Outside a large metropolitan city in a quiet residential area, lives a woman with a beautiful spirit. She has been given a most extraordinary gift. She has been given the gift of healing by the laying on of hands and she is working miracles. Not surprisingly, her reputation is growing. This chapter was written by Terry, whereby she tells about healing from her own perspective.

To those who believe in spiritual healing, no explanation is necessary. To those who do not believe, no explanation is possible. It is not my desire to convince anyone of anything, or to convert anyone to any belief system other than what they now follow. You are exactly where you need to be according to your awareness at this moment. If you find yourself reading

1

this book, I ask only that you accept that which rings true to your inner being. For the remainder of the material, set it aside on the back shelf of your mind until such time that you have an experience which relates to it. It is very difficult to believe without personal experience. Do not totally discard anything as impossible because you personally lack an experience which relates to it; likewise, it would be equally foolish to wholeheartedly accept something which does not resonate in truth with something deep within yourself.

It is not solely the personality, the mortal self that you see in the healer or in the person healed that does this work of healing. It is a much larger, truer and deeper self that is in operation when healing occurs. It is the spirit, the divinity within, the God within that works through universal forces and triggers self-healing.

We have all heard the term psychosomatic, referring to the effect that the mind has on the physical body. In reality, the issue is more truthfully stated when one refers to spirit, mind and body. It is a great fallacy to overlook spirit when considering the state of the mind and the body. They are inseparable and disturbance in one area is reflected in all three sooner or later; usually sooner.

You may not be ready for this message at this time. Yet again, it may strike a clear note of intuition deep within yourself. Personally, I feel no need to attempt to authenticate any of these experiences included in this book because it is of no consequence to me whether or not we have the appropriate instrumentation to measure these subtle yet profound healing energies. It suffices me that it simply works. Several years ago, an engineer with a very impressive background and credentials came from Washington D.C., and requested to study me and the energy conducting through me. Reluctantly, I agreed but I felt it was a waste of my time and in the end the answer would elude him. The answer lies in the unified field of awareness and we have no subtle energy recording device to measure this spectrum. We worked together for three years. He asked endless questions and I answered them, as he repeatedly experienced the energy coming through my hands to him. He was never able to measure or record this energy, but three years later, he was a fine healer in addition to being a successful engineer. He knows now that healing is an intuitive natural ability to attract energies, transform them with very little conscious effort, and transmit them to another person to induce self-healing. All healing is self-healing. No one heals another person against their will. One cannot measure the energy, but can definitely observe and measure the results by conventional methods.

During a healing session, I do not depend totally on rational decision making or some preplanned procedure. There are many factors involved in healing that go far beyond the scope of any technique. There is very little analyzing and intellectualizing at the conscious level. It is more important for me to be totally relaxed and yet quietly focused on what is happening. Keen observation and an intuitive knowing guide me to respond effectively to the slightest nuance. My mind is very still and at peace, enabling me to detect the slightest change of variation at the onset. The entire healing session is determined by those signals which I am receiving and responding to. This level of consciousness is almost impossible to verbally describe.

3

Anyone who has experienced it will realize the hands can sense with as much accuracy as the eyes can see and frequently with far more detail.

Dr. Todd Dixon has made a great effort to interview all the people involved in each case and carefully study their medical records and medical findings. You are free to accept or reject anything recorded herein. He has worked diligently to present these happenings to you exactly as they occurred. Even as he shares this material with you, I know that it represents a small shadow of the source from which it sprang. Some readers will have a certain insight into these matters and others will be totally blind. It is my sincere wish that you will extract from this book that which is most helpful to you.

We have left many fascinating events out of the book, in order to keep our focus of attention on the physical conditions that were healed. In working with healing, one naturally touches on other areas of the human condition and the human psyche in its relationship to the universe as a whole. We are not isolated little beings, but a part of the whole, a part of all that is. We are multi-dimentional to an extent that almost staggers the imagination.

The body consists of many subtle energies that can be altered and affected by other energies. At some time in the not too distant future, the body will be regarded as more electrical than chemical. Love, fear, hatred, guilt (justified or unjustified) and an endless array of emotions are actually energy in motion. Look at the word e-motion. This energy in motion has a tremendous effect on our spirit, mind and body. The bottom line is that it can make or break us.

Often, we bring suffering, pain and distress into our own lives because it serves as a warning or a wake-up call. Our lives have become so unraveled that we are coming apart at the seams. The pain and distress signals that we must reevaluate our life situation and reset ourselves and our life situations, if we plan to survive and live. At times, people can sink so low into a particular illness that they do not have the strength to pull themselves up by the bootstraps. Thus, outside help becomes a necessity. Some form of outside intervention becomes imperative to interrupt the unfortunate negative state of the physical or emotional condition. There are many modalities of healing. If the condition has progressed to a certain level, surgery may be indicated. At this point, medication may also prove helpful. I am not advocating the use of unnecessary drugs, but medication has its proper use. It is erroneous to feel that one must go to extremes and select only spiritual healing or medical treatment. They are very compatible and can enhance each other.

Many of the people who come to me also see a psychiatrist. The spiritual healing is especially effective in recovering the repressed subconscious. As the healing causes these hidden traumas to surface, it is processed and dealt with in therapy. This is also a compatible arrangement. In many cases, the healing suffices, but in other instances another form of assistance will greatly speed the recovery process. Frequently, the condition has deteriorated to such an extent that time is of the essence to preserve life. I work with many high risk pregnancy cases and the healing has tremendous impact on the person. It allays the fears and provides a sense of tranquility and security unsurpassed by any tranquilizer. Obviously, this does not substitute for any part of the prenatal care provided by the obstetrician.

When one considers the phenomenon of healing with energies, whether it is by placing the hands on the body or by magnetic passes over the body, one must take into consideration many other factors. The rapport between healer and the person to be healed is very significant, and cannot be ignored. The personality of the healer must be such that it is totally non-threatening, and leaves the person with a feeling of unconditional love and a sense of security. It requires great courage for some people to seek out a healer, because they are facing what is unknown to them. Although the healer works every day with the healing energies, the healer can never afford to overlook the fact that it is a new experience for the person who is about to receive a healing. Healing is not related to time or space. The healer needs to explain very carefully to the person receiving the healing that the condition may be handled in one session; then again, it may require more than one healing to complete the recovery. I find, in general, if the condition has been chronic, it requires a few sessions. A condition which has only recently manifested itself can be dealt with more quickly. For instance, nightmares in children usually require only one session of healing and the nightmares cease. In adults, however, one healing session sometimes does not suffice to eliminate the nightmares, because underlying conditions which are long-standing have produced them. These under-lying conditions and contributing factors must be healed first, then the nightmares will cease.

It is also a fact that one person will be healed more quickly with one healer than another. This may be explained by the compatibility of energy ranges within the healer and the person to be healed. On occasion, when I am encountering an experience for the first time, my body experiences a sensation of becoming accustomed to a new frequency of energy. It is a subtle sensation, but it does reach my conscious awareness. When this same type of encounter occurs on subsequent occasions, I do not sense it in an isolated way. It is as if my body can now automatically regulate this current of energy without conscious awareness.

Many people ask how I get this energy to flow through my hands. I simply pray for that which is most beneficial for this particular person to flow through my hands. My orientation is first and foremost spiritual. Without the spirit, the little ego or personality is capable of using only a minute fraction of the power of the mind. With spirit, the mind opens onto a limitless field of possibilities. When we operate from ego alone, depending on our dubious intellectualizing based on our limited training, we disconnect ourselves from the source. When the spirit is engaged, then the mind can operate with full and limitless possibilities. It is an automatic process and can attract any solution to any situation. If we attempt to think it through with the conscious intellect we stop the direct knowledge flow with our feeble attempt to control things. Many people are so locked into this limited position of intellectualizing that they cannot comprehend or even imagine that there is a universe beyond this. I have witnessed the results so many times that for me it cannot even be labeled as faith. It is an inner knowing that has no seed of doubt. My personality and little ego can make no claims. The results occur as a direct result from opening onto something which is much greater than my little self.

It is also not possible to heal anyone against their free will. Unfortunately, some decide that it would be better to check out on life, because they perceive their situation to be overwhelming or too much effort to confront. People tell me this honestly and directly. Sometimes, if there is a shred of willingness, they can be healed of this hopelessness. The point is that an interaction occurs and it does require, at least, the cooperation of the person to be healed. With this cooperation and willingness to be well, all things are possible. In order to be healed, one does not require a belief in healing or in the healer. It is very acceptable to say "I am very skeptical." There is no reason to wholeheartedly believe something of which you have no experience. Skeptics are healed. Unwillingness and utter resistance prove to be obstacles that are insurmountable.

Religion is another question that is often raised. I simply believe in the Brotherhood of man and the Fatherhood of God, and as such I work with people of all races, colors and creeds. I know from having traveled to every continent on earth that there are many fine healers from all religions. The subject addresses itself to spirituality and not to specific religions.

Another question frequently asked is "Can one be trained to be a healer?" We all have the potential, but in some the potential is far greater than in others. I believe it is much like training an opera singer; if he is born with the voice then it can be trained. There are many who have the capacity to be healers and are unaware of it, simply because of a lack of exposure to the experience of healing through natural energies. First and foremost, the selection of a student requires that he or she have an adequate level of development; otherwise, giving knowledge is a fruitless procedure, because he or she cannot apply the knowledge in a useful way. In order to expand the level of development, I teach an unconditional type of meditation. Thus, the student must be disciplined enough to faithfully meditate at least twice a day on his own to insure an expanding awareness and a level of stability. The student receives healing, so that he knows from experience what takes place and healing serves as a purification. If the healer is not clear, then exhaustion occurs readily. In the worst scenario he will take onto himself others' ailments.

It is wise to be cautious and adequately prepared before working on others and it is of extreme importance to work on oneself first. When the student is selected, meditating on a regular basis and receiving healing and purification, then knowledge can be imparted. The student is now ready to work with the healer, apprentice-style, to gain a repertoire of experience before going out on his own. This method seems to produce capable and secure healers. Sincerity and dedication must be ever present.

For me, healing is a lifestyle and cannot be done on an eight hours a day basis. I find it necessary to pray and meditate to stay attuned and balanced. Balance in one's life cannot be overestimated where healing is concerned. It is not a question of more, more and more meditating or anything else, but a constant watch over the balance of all facets of life. A simple lifestyle without unnecessary, self-created turmoil aids the healer in maintaining a quiet mind with single-pointed focus of attention on the task at hand. Occasionally, I fast and find this beneficial in purging both the body and mind. Moderation and simplicity are excellent guidelines in eating, sleeping, working and recreation. It is wise to avoid noise pollution as this is devastating to concentration and serenity, and destroys the delicate balance in the healer. This results in a scattering of vital energies and disconnects you from the deep intuitive wisdom of the life forces. It is difficult for me to explain in linguistically structured thoughts the spontaneity which I find necessary to healing, because it does not involve conscious rational processes. I trust that the reader will understand what I am saying in the absence of appropriate descriptive terms.

We stand on the brink of a very interesting and exciting time. So much is available to us that has not been provided for any previous generation. Let us open our minds to ever widening possibilities and throw off the shackles which create our own self-imposed limitations. There are many healers and many different methods of healing. There is no single correct method. Healing can occur through prayer, meditation, wisdom, love, laughter, by using herbs and plants, through foods and through abstaining from foods. There are endless possibilities for healing all around us. Seek that which is most beneficial to you. Undergo intense self-examination and determine what is your message in life, then attempt to live your own message.

Life is an ever changing process, an ongoing transformation. If we are to remain healthy, we must flow with the changes. Stagnation occurs when we block the flow of life forces, and this obstruction and static condition result in disease. Frequently, healing is secondary to a change in consciousness. If healing is accomplished and the attitude which brought on disease is not changed, then the same condition will be recreated. Healing concerns the most important relationship of all: your relationship with yourself.

In a small residential area outside of the city of Dakar in Senegal, North Africa, I received healing from a Senegalese man. He didn't utter a single word during the entire procedure. He worked with his hands at a distance of ten to twelve inches from the surface of my body. His only communication with me was a quiet smile that said, "Hello, come in and there is nothing to fear." Thirty days after he nodded his head in farewell, I was still feeling the effects of his healing. Ten years have passed since that visit, but when I hear the word Africa, I still experience the gentle, all-pervading, divine, impersonal love which emanated through him. A similiar experience happened in New York with an old Japanese woman who spoke no English just as I spoke no Japanese. A simple bow said "We are about to begin," and another simple bow said "The healing is done." All that remains with me is the incredible power of her impersonal love and concern for well-being. I am enriched for having interacted with these two people. It has been my great fortune to have touched the lives briefly of two Tibetan monks whose gifts to me could never be measured.

In conclusion, I would like to share with you a typical healing from beginning to end. First, the person to receive healing must request the healing for himself and make his own appointment, unless the person is a child, in which case a parent speaks on his behalf. An exception is also made for someone who is too ill to make his own arrangements. Secondly, I speak to the person and explain to the best of my ability what is about to happen. A healing session is not related to time. The person to be healed lies on a comfortable bed, and then I kneel down and begin praying silently, asking God to heal the person. Initially, my left arm is raised with my palm facing upwards. This hand receives the healing energy. My right hand is placed over the person's head and it is my right hand that transmits the energy to the patient. I then place my hands on either side of the person's head and transmit the energy to his brain. My hands are held about 1 to 2 inches above the skin. This is very important in the healing, because it is the brain which controls the entire body. The rest of the healing I work mainly with the person's energy field. (See human energy field in the chapter on Research.)

My hands are very sensitive to this field of energy and give knowledge I need during a healing. I can feel where the person has had surgery without seeing the scar. Many times the aura will show the area that contains disease. Then I work on that part of the aura (energy field) that is diseased. Change the energy field and you can change the diseased physical body. It is also important to balance the energy and recharge the chakras. (Chakras are vortexes of energy within the human energy field.) If I have been working on a person who has hepatitis, the high vibrational energy will be concentrated at the liver. The healing process is greatly enhanced when the subtle energies are balanced throughout the body and the human energy field. At the end of the healing, my hands are magnetically passed 2 to 12 inches above the person's body which allows all the energies of the body to be uniformly distributed and balanced. Sometimes the healing is over in five minutes, while another may take an hour. It depends on what transpires.

During a healing there is frequently a sensation of sinking or floating slightly or both sensations alternating with each other during the sessions. The person receiving healing is encouraged to talk if he so desires, to ask any questions or to remain in total silence if he is more comfortable with that. Much of the stress that leaves during healing, whether it is physical, mental or emotional, bypasses the conscious mind. The only indication that stress has been released is that the person feels more relaxed, an increasing sense of comfort and an improved overall sense of well-being with the cessation of pain. When the person sits up after healing, there is a momentary lightheadedness which is alleviated in approximately two minutes. The lightheadedness is due to healing in the head and is readily dispersed by using magnetic passes over the body to bring about a grounding effect. The final portion of the healing consists of answering any questions which may arise or dealing with any trauma which may have surfaced. During the healing, the person is usually awake and alert, but sometimes too relaxed to converse. Talking just seems to be too much of an effort under such relaxed conditions. Some momentarily drop off to sleep. Before bidding the person farewell and dismissing him, I explain some possible side effects of the healing. They include frequent urination, short-term diarrhea, night sweating, the need for extra sleep, coughing up mucous from the lungs, watering eyes, and slight twitches in the muscles in any area of the body. All of the above mentioned are simply the body's own natural methods of releasing toxins and purifying the body. It is important to explain these healing effects to the person, otherwise he will mistake frequent urination following healing as some distress in the urinary system and seek medication for what is in reality the body healing itself.

Healing energy frequently manifests as light. Some people can actually see the light. Usually, it occurs so fast that it is all over before the person realizes it. There is no fear because the display of light is over before realization of it occurs. Healing energy is light and light travels; thus, healing can be sent over great distance. Healing is beyond time and space. As a matter of fact, there is a time warp during healing. Frequently, an hour passes and seems to be only five or ten minutes. There is also a sound warp, which magnifies sound. If the telephone rings while you are fully awake, it is not shattering, but during healing a silence sets in which magnifies the sound of the phone, because of the relative silence. The body becomes so quiet and relaxed that the heart can easily be heard. Healing energy also has a typical high-pitched sound. It is most unlikely that any one person would by aware of all these occurrences, because they are very subtle. Different people pick up on different aspects of healing.

I fully realize that my words do not begin to scratch the surface of healing in general, and only represent a slight reflection of the area in which I work. There is no one single approach that is better than another. Each healer develops the technique that is most natural and comfortable to him. The real essence of healing comes from a common source to which we all have access. It is my wish that you have found something in these words that will be thought provoking and thus enrich your life. May you tap into the source and attract into your life the love, the joy and the good health that you so richly deserve.

CHAPTER TWO
INFERTILITY

Despite years of trying and longing for a child, my wife and I were unable to conceive. When we originally saw a physician about our infertility, we were told the prognosis was poor. We wanted our own child so much that we would do whatever we could medically to optimize our chances of having our own child. Surgery and medical procedures were both necessary to optimize our chances. However, we still could not conceive a child.

A good friend of mine told me about a healer. I was curious more than anything else. Although I believed in healing and that certain people had been given this gift, I wanted to see if this person was authentic.

My first appointment with Terry was a unique experience. I would describe her as having a heart of gold. She was delighted to carry on a conversation before the healing, and I found her to be friendly and intelligent. She claimed to have a 50% success rate with couples who have not conceived a child despite the help of infertility specialists.

I was a little out of balance. Although I had not drunk since college, I felt like I had awakened on a Saturday morning after drinking on a Friday night. As a matter of fact, I had felt out of balance (polluted) for most of my stay in the big city, where I was living to complete my medical training.

Terry took me upstairs and had me lie on a bed. She then covered my eyes with a soft cloth, so I couldn't see. I next felt her hands near my head and it felt as if her hands were producing considerable heat. I became very relaxed as she moved her hands to different parts of my body.

At the end of the healing, which lasted close to a half an hour, I was extremely relaxed and revitalized. The polluted feeling was gone and I was left with a sense of peace and well-being. It was wonderful. It was also remarkable how I felt at work. Being an anesthesiologist, I have to deal with a great deal of stress, sharp tempers and negativity. After the healing with Terry, I was immune to the negative work environment. I was at peace, and nothing said by the surgeon nor anyone else in the operating room could upset me. It must have appeared as if I were on valium, but valium can dull the senses and my senses were clear.

I made an appointment for my wife with Terry, and we continued to see the infertility specialists, and do everything medically possible to have our own child. After two months my wife conceived. My wife and I were elated.

My wife was 36 years old and we had some talk about amniocentesis, which is usually recommended for women over 35 years of age to test for genetic defects. We considered a new procedure, chorionic villi sampling (cvs), which is similiar to amniocentesis, but can be performed earlier in pregnancy. The risk of either one of these procedures is miscarriage. My wife and I were unsure of what to do. We did not want our child to suffer if there were a genetic abnormality; however, my wife felt the baby was normal. We had waited so long for this child, we didn't want to risk losing this pregnancy. After lengthy discussions my wife had the cvs performed. When we received the results of the cvs we were once again elated. The tests showed no genetic defects for our baby girl.

Soon after the cvs was performed, my wife felt a little abdominal discomfort, like gas pains. Later on she noticed spotting. That night the bed was full of blood and by morning the fetus was aborted.

My wife grieved for weeks and then became depressed. She had a strong feeling that the abortion was caused by the cvs. In the midst of her depression she felt there must be something she had to learn from this. "What is it?"

I consoled my wife with my belief that we had not lost our girl in the miscarriage. I believed we would have her same spirit in a future pregnancy or be with her in the hereafter.

We again did everything we could to conceive a child. We tried to maintain a positive mental attitude. We continued to see the infertility specialists along with their special procedures, and we continued to see Terry. It was not as easy the second time around. After a number of months of trying without success the infertility specialists began discussing options, which included not having our own child. This was disheartening to us, but we did not lose hope.

The next healing was the week before Christmas, and during my healing Terry said there was a "very high vibrational energy (spirit) in the room." She left me alone in the room with this energy. Gloria, my wife, had her healing a few days after mine and again Terry stated there was a "very high vibrational energy (spirit) in the room." Terry told my wife that the conditions for a successful pregnancy were optimum and left the room, leaving Gloria alone with this energy. The week after Christmas my wife conceived.

My wife was now 37 years old and her doctor recommended she have an amniocentesis. Needless to say we were not thrilled by this recommmendation. I did not believe that God would give us a child with a genetic defect. Maybe that's what God wanted us to learn; he wanted us to place our trust in him. We believed our unborn child was healthy and didn't want the test done. My wife wanted Terry's opinion. Terry also felt this was a test of faith. She prayed for Gloria to have a dream, which would help her in making her decision.

A couple of nights later Gloria had a dream, and saw a little girl standing at the feet of someone. She could not see the face of this person, but he appeared to be a "star figure." Gloria was crying because she thought the child had a genetic defect. To Gloria's surprise the little girl turned around and was a perfectly normal pretty girl!

Gloria opted not to have any genetic testing done

and to leave this in the hands of the Lord. Anxiety was the theme of my wife's pregnancy. The only thing that seemed to help was a positive mental attitude that God would give us a normal child. Indeed, on September 20, 1989 Gloria did give birth to a normal, healthy, beautiful, brown-eyed girl! It's difficult for me to describe the joy I have received from our daughter, Michelle Christina Dixon. It's also difficult for me to describe the feelings that come over me when I see her giggling in the morning or I'm kissing her to sleep at night. It's hard to imagine going through life without her. I do know that she is a living testament to me each day of my life, a testament to the powerful combination of our medical technology, faith and the healing power.

CHAPTER THREE
BREAST CANCER

In the spring of 1987, Trudy Hall went to see her gynecologist because she had discovered a lump in her breast. The gynecologist told her that it was fibrocystic disease and that it was nothing to worry about. This did not allay her anxiety. One month later, after a second examination, Trudy's gynecologist again stated she had fibrocystic disease. Despite the reassurance, Trudy's anxiety persisted. By the end of the summer Trudy's breast was red and swollen. Realizing something was wrong, she made an appointment with a general surgeon. After examination he gave Trudy the bad news. He told her she had a very serious condition and the prognosis was not good. The surgeon scheduled Trudy for a breast biopsy, but was sure she had inoperable breast cancer. Trudy knew this too.

She was devastated. Distraught and in tears, she

broke the news to her husband that night. Her husband, Mike Hall, was always the stronger of the two. However, he was also overwhelmed with the knowledge that his wife had inoperable breast cancer.

Mike Hall had been a priest at one time and he began to pray. He prayed for his wife's life. That evening he told his story to an acquaintance, a construction worker. The construction worker told him of a healer who had helped him. Mike wrote down Terry's name and phone number.

The next morning Trudy called Terry. It was a Saturday, and like every Saturday it was extremely busy for Terry. Although she had been booked full, she found the time to fit Trudy in.

During the first healing, Trudy was distraught, crying, desperate, physically and emotionally exhausted. She had not slept in three days. She did not remember very much of the healing. All that she remembered was going downstairs after the healing, lying on Terry's couch and falling asleep.

Trudy made an appointment with a general surgeon at a leading university hospital. Surgery and medical workup indicated she had inoperable breast cancer. The general surgeon told Trudy she had a 30% chance of living for 5 years if she underwent chemotherapy and it was successful. He also explained that he couldn't operate at this time, but if she responded to chemotherapy he might be able to operate at a later date.

Trudy was referred to an oncologist for chemotherapy. Her therapy consisted of two weeks on the drugs adriamycin, cytoxan, and 5-FU and then off the drugs for two weeks. Trudy was told that she would be on this regimen for a full year.

Trudy continued to see Terry each week, and progressively felt more and more optimistic about her prognosis. During the healings she did not describe any intensely spiritual experience, such as an out of the body experience or vivid whirling lights. But she did feel what almost everyone feels during a healing; HEAT. Trudy felt considerable heat in her right breast (the one with the cancer.) During the next week Trudy continued to feel the effects of the healing. She felt like there was a war being fought in her right breast. "It was as if the healthy part of my body was fighting the unhealthy cancer cells." In addition, Terry gave Trudy inspirational healing tapes by Louise Hayes to listen to.

There was no sudden enlightenment or drastic improvement. There was, however, a gradual change of attitude. Trudy began to feel deep down inside that she would be all right. There was a peace that overcame her. In the midst of chemotherapy and fighting cancer, this was the most peaceful she had ever been in her life.

The oncologist treating Trudy had informed her that she would be losing her hair, as well as having other side effects of chemotherapy. She didn't. Each time she returned to his office with a full head of hair he would reassure her that her hair would probably fall out. Each time she returned to his office he was amazed that she had not lost her hair. The oncologist told her that it was cases like hers that kept him humble.

By winter, Trudy had responded so well to chemotherapy that her surgeon told her the cancer was now operable, and she was scheduled for surgery. The nurses in the surgeon's office remarked upon how well Trudy looked. She didn't look like a cancer patient; she looked healthy.

Trudy had a modified radical mastectomy. Her surgeon stated after the surgery, "I was amazed at what I found. It looked as if a battle had taken place in her breast. Even more striking, her breast tissue was like no other tissue I had seen before. It felt like some type of gluey substance, which made it very difficult to handle." Because of the gluey texture of the breast tissue the surgery took 5 hours, much longer than usual. The surgeon told Trudy's family it was the best response to chemotherapy he had ever seen. Prognosis was excellent for Trudy.

Today Trudy is much more optimistic, spiritual and doesn't take life for granted. Trudy has been cancer free for five years. Although surgery and chemotherapy were definite cornerstones of her therapy, she feels it was the healing power that was 70% responsible for her cure.

CHAPTER FOUR
HEART DISEASE

Mike Hall was a Catholic priest for 8 years, so he was somewhat familiar with healing by the laying on of hands. Mike performed the laying on of hands for many people in his church and believes some of them were healed. However, he was unfamiliar with professional healers or people who have dedicated their lives to healing.

Mike was the husband of Trudy Hall (see Breast Cancer) and was overwhelmed when his wife informed him she had inoperable breast cancer. Distraught and on the verge of despair, he began to pray for his wife's life. That night he told his friend that his wife had inoperable breast cancer. His friend told him of someone who had helped him and might be able to help his wife. Crying, despondent and willing to try almost anything, he wrote down Terry's name and phone number.

Mike saw Terry because his wife was seeing her, and not for any physical problems he had. He considered himself fairly healthy; however, on a routine annual insurance checkup he was found to have an abnormal EKG (electrocardiogram). To be more specific he had a left bundle branch block. In layman's terms, the heart has specialized nerve pathways that cause the heart to beat in a synchronized manner. The synchronicity of these specialized pathways is tested by an electrocardiogram. The specialized pathway starts out as one single bundle of specialized nerves, then branches out repeatedly so that these specialized nerves are dispersed throughout the heart. One of the main branches of specialized nerve fibers in Mike's heart was blocked or no longer working. This usually signals an underlying heart disease, which required Mike to have a full work up of his heart. A stress test and coronary angiogram were performed, and found to be normal. The only thing found to be abnormal was a consistent finding of left bundle branch block. The records were sent to me, Dr. Dixon, and I have verified the results of these tests.

Mike's cardiologist (heart doctor) said he would probably have this left bundle branch block the rest of his life. After several healings with Terry, a followup electrocardiogram was normal, with no evidence of left bundle branch block. This electrocardiogram was also sent to me, and I have verified that it is normal.

Being a Catholic priest for eight years, Mike probably had more faith than your average American. This background may have let Mike have experiences during his healings that other people may never experience. Again, what is most consistently striking was the radiation of heat from Terry's hands. Mike experienced vivid bright colors, much brighter and more vivid than colors we see day to day. He experienced complete calm, inner peace and at times the feeling that he was outside of his body. What impressed Mike the most was how Terry would accurately describe what he was feeling and experiencing.

Before one healing Mike was feeling stressed-out from work and problems encountered in everyday life. During the initial part of healing Mike was nervous, fidgety and felt numb, almost as if he was wrapped in cellophane. All of a sudden the barrier broke and he felt that God was with him in the room. Again Mike was impressed with how Terry accurately described what he felt and experienced.

Mike was also bothered by a torn muscle in the back of his thigh, which caused considerable pain when walking. He had not been able to run for months. During a healing session Mike experienced pain exactly where the torn muscle was. Terry told him he was feeling the healing energy working on his torn muscle. The next day Mike began running with only minor discomfort.

Although he was already a strong believer in Christ, God and the Catholic faith, Mike feels that he is much more spiritual now as a result of healings and meditation (as taught to him by Terry) than he was as a Catholic priest.

CHAPTER FIVE
CROSS-EYED

Tom Hall, son of Trudy Hall, was born with severe strabismus. Strabismus in layman's terms means cross-eyed. Instead of the eyes looking straight ahead, they either look toward each other or away from each other. In Tom's case his eyes looked away from each other. The ophthomologist (eye doctor) said that Tom was also far-sighted, which often occurs with strabismus.

Tom had surgery when he was three years old to correct the strabismus. The surgery only corrected 85% of the strabismus, which meant that the eyes still looked away from each other and Tom's far-sightedness remained. The ophthomologist told Mrs. Hall that Tom would probably have to wear corrective eye glasses until he was ten years old, and that his far-sightedness was never expected to be totally corrected. Tom had to wear what was described by his family and friends as coke bottle glasses, because the lenses were so thick.

When Tom was five and half years old, Mrs. Hall took him to see Terry. On those days when Terry was not available, Mary (Terry's student) would give Tom a healing. To Trudy Hall's amazement, Tom's eyesight gradually improved. Tom did not describe what he felt during these healings, however, one healing was noteworthy to Mrs. Hall. According to Mrs. Hall "It was as if Tom had been hit by a bolt of lightning. He was dizzy and couldn't walk straight. When we arrived home he went to bed and fell into a deep sleep." Mary (Terry's student) had felt tremendous energy during the healings she performed on Tom.

When Tom was seven and a half years old, Mrs. Hall noticed that Tom's eyes were watering after a healing. Trudy Hall took Tom to the ophthomologist, and according to Trudy Hall, the ophthomologist was amazed that Tom's vision was now 20/20 (he was no longer far-sighted) and he no longer had strabismus.

Tom's family had a party to celebrate Tom's new vision. Friends, family and relatives were amazed to see that Tom no longer had to wear coke bottle glasses. The highlight of the party was Tom taking his glasses and smashing them to pieces.

CHAPTER SIX
FOOT PAIN

Susan Jennings was born with a foot disorder. She had extremely high arches and hammer toes, which caused excruciating pain when walking. Despite physical therapy and specially designed shoes, nothing seemed to help the pain.

Susan was referred to Terry by her daughter, who had been helped by Terry. Susan received healings once every three weeks. She described these healings as a state of extreme relaxation, floating at times, with waves of electricity flooding her body. Over the course of six to eight months Susan gradually improved to the point where she only had minor discomfort when walking. The podiatrist stated that he had never seen her feet in better condition.

Susan also received other benefits from the healings. Susan had an extreme fear of flying, or more appropriately terror. She wouldn't travel by plane. She was also plagued by claustrophobia (fear of closed places), stemming from having a fire in her house when she was a young child. Whenever Susan and her husband went to the movies, it made Susan extremely uneasy. Susan would have to sit on the aisle seat or near an exit. Needless to say, the claustrophobia was not limited to movie theatres.

Since the healings with Terry, Susan no longer has a fear of flying. She even travels in small planes. She is no longer claustrophobic and handles stress and everyday life much better. "Terry has helped me in so many ways, and very importantly, has also given me good common sense."

CHAPTER SEVEN
ARTHRITIS

Athletic and muscle bound, Phil was not always in good shape. His parents were born and raised in Europe, during times when food and money were not easy to come by. His parents nearly starved. However, times changed after they came to America. With the memory of the scarcity of money and food, his parents were amazed at the results of American free enterprise. There was a sense of gratification to have well fed children. Phil was fed so well, however, that he was nicknamed "fatso."

Phil had a complex about being fat and being nicknamed "fatso." He discovered that he didn't have to be fat if he didn't want to be. He was lured to athletics and the martial arts, and was gratified by his new physique. However, he was not easy on his new body; in fact, it may be more properly termed abuse. Twenty three years in the martial arts, power lifting, poor posture and hours of sitting at a desk took an incredible toll on Phil's body. He began having pain and stiffness in his joints, which eventually incapacitated him and he sought medical attention.

Phil was found to have osteoarthritis, a condition caused by repetitive trauma to the joints. He was treated with anti-inflammatory drugs, which helped ameliorate the pain, but not the progression of his disease. He soon developed numbness in his hands and experienced difficulty walking and buttoning his shirt. The trigger which sent Phil to the hospital was tripping over an extension cord at a supermarket. This event left him temporarily paralyzed and incapacitated by unbearable pain.

The medical records were sent to me and I have verified the reports. MRI (a radiological picture similiar to the CAT scan, but giving higher resolution of the picture) showed severe degenerative arthritis of the spine in Phil's neck and upper back. Bone and fibrous tissue of the spine were impinging upon the nerves as they left the spinal canal. The surgeons told Phil that he needed immediate surgery, or paralysis of his arms and legs or even death might result.

The surgeons performed surgery on the spine of Phil's neck. The operation was a success, but he had a residual numbness in both arms after surgery. The neurologists (doctors of the brain and nerves) informed Phil they could not guarantee that sensation would return to his arms, and that he would almost definitely need another surgery. These comments made to Phil, were not documented in the medical records.

Phil was referred to Terry by his daughter, because of her own success with the healing treatments. Phil, being macho and extremely skeptical, was reluctant to go. It was only after repetitive coersion that he agreed to see Terry.

During the healings with Terry, Phil felt tremendous heat radiate from Terry's hands, and heard growling in his stomach and intestines. He felt a sensation like sinking into a deep, black hole. A wonderful feeling of floating or being outside of his body overcame him. During one of Phil's healings he was told by Terry that his numbness would go away within the month. Over the next two weeks Phil's numbness gradually improved, then one night the sensation in both arms suddenly "flooded back." There was complete recovery of sensation.

Terry also taught Phil how to meditate, overcome guilt and she gave him an uncanny sense of optimism. Phil now feels that he handles stress incredibly well, much better than before he met Terry.

CHAPTER EIGHT
PROSTATE CANCER

In January of 1989, Steve developed a bladder infection and consulted a urologist. The urologist felt an abnormal consistency when examining Steve's prostate and recommended a biopsy.

When Steve was told that he had cancer his initial response was panic, or more appropriately termed terror. The terror soon became sadness and loneliness. It was striking how alone he felt. "It was as if no one cared as deeply about my condition as I did, and the proof was that they (family and friends) were going about their lives as though nothing had happened!" Steve became very angry that no one seemed to care as much as he thought they would care. However, "in the midst of anger" Steve was taught a very valuable lesson. "The lesson was simply that I, and only I, am totally concerned with my life and I alone, of all the people in the universe, must do what I need to do for myself. No one else can do that."

Steve researched and read everything he could a-
bout prostate cancer, including a 300 page set of
printouts from a medical data bank. He arranged to see
another urologist at a leading U.S. hospital for cancer
patients. The urologist told Steve he had three options,
since the cancer had not spread beyond the prostate
gland itself. The three options were either surgery,
radiation or wait and see what happens. Steve was
amazed that he had the option of taking no aggressive
therapy at this time. So Steve asked a logical question.
"Is it possible that the cancer will go away?" The
oncologist's firm reply was "No."

Steve decided to go with no medical treatment. He
did not know whether he could beat the cancer
without medical treatment, especially after what he
was told by the oncologist. He had heard numerous
stories of people who had, and he thought it was worth
a try. Steve purchased every self-help book he could
read on beating cancer, and the underlying theme was
a positive mental attitude. He attended the Lawrence
LeShan workshop to reinforce that positive attitude.
Steve "learned about the importance of 'singing my
own song' as a way to stimulate and assist my immune
system. This gives maximum support to my body and
to whatever medical treatment I would be receiving."
The workshop is designed to take your life goals and
actualize them.

Steve began to actualize his goals of writing. Steve
wrote a book, which was his dream for many years.
When he could not find a publisher, Steve undertook
the complex task involved in self-publishing. His work
appeared in print a year later.

Steve found out about Terry through his wife's friend, who was receiving healings by Terry. He was skeptical that someone could heal by the laying on of hands, but very open to trying. He was by no means certain that this would help.

When Steve entered Terry's home, he was very unimpressed by her office, "for it was not an office at all. It was simply her home and the healing was done on her bed." Steve was surprised that the healer did not have any extravagant equipment to work with. During the first healing session, Steve felt a vibrating warmth from Terry's hands, as though "they were vibrating very fast," and he entered an altered state. It wasn't a hypnotic state, for he had been hypnotized before; this was different. He felt something significant was happening and this quickened his interest. After two to three healings, Steve was no longer skeptical. He did not know if the healings would help cure his cancer, and quite frankly he simply avoided the question. This was something important and he was going to finish it.

Steve continued to see Terry every week for six months. Terry felt that Steve was very receptive to the healings, possibly because of his training in yoga, meditation and many years of compassionate Gestalt psychotherapy. Steve was excited about what was happening to him and had an inner sense that things would be all right. When I asked Steve if the healings gave him inner calm, he replied, "No." He felt a tremendous surge of energy during the healings. To help himself deal with this surge of energy he started smoking again, after having quit years before.

Steve always felt something was supporting him. During one healing session, Steve felt there was something in the room. There was a light and the face of Jesus appeared. Steve spoke to him asking for forgiveness, and Jesus stated "of course you're forgiven." This happened during another healing, and the vividness and quality of the experience convinced Steve it was real. Being Jewish, Steve told some of his Jewish friends of his experience, and he was sharply criticized. "How can you believe in Jesus!?" they exclaimed. And yet, he saw what he saw.

To his own and his doctors' amazement, Steve has been free of prostate cancer for the past three years. He attributes his ability to beating cancer to many factors, including: a positive mental attitude, the LeShan workshop, and completing and publishing his own book. However, he considers the healings by Terry to be the keystone in the doorway holding up all the other stones. Steve said, "They all came together to help me beat the cancer, but it was the healings that appeared to be the most significant piece."

CHAPTER NINE
HEPATITIS

Jim is in his twenties and uses drugs, at times I.V. drugs. He was never able to kick the habit, and finally one of the complications of I.V. drug use occurred.

Jim began to complain of abdominal pain. He became lethargic, looked ill and finally his abdominal pain became so severe that he was forced to see a doctor. Blood work was drawn at the doctor's office, but there was little doubt of the diagnosis after history taking and physical examination by the physician. On physical examination Jim had an enlarged tender liver and yellow eyes (jaundice). Jim had hepatitis. Specifically Non-A Non-B Hepatitis, an extremely serious inflammation of the liver (sometimes fatal) caused by a virus transmitted by I.V. drug use. The liver enzyme levels came back in the thousands, indicating a very serious infection.

The prognosis (outcome) varies with hepatitis; some patients recover completely, some develop chronic persistent hepatitis (the liver never returns to normal, but the patient usually returns to a normal lifestyle). Some develop chronic active hepatitis (inflammation of the liver persists, liver damage continues, and outcome is usually not good) and some patients die.

The doctor's prognosis for Jim was a prolonged recovery. His doctor felt it would be months (usually it takes 3-6 months) before Jim would feel better again. Jim's mother recommended he see a healer, as she had been doing. Having an open mind, Jim agreed.

One week later Jim saw Terry. During the healing Jim felt heat radiating from Terry's hands. The heat could be felt upon his head and seemed to be entering his eyes. When Terry's hands were over Jim's liver dramatic changes occurred. He could feel the energy enter his liver and shortly thereafter he became short of breath. When he mentioned this to Terry, she said this was caused by the healing energy enlarging the liver which was now pressing against his lungs, causing the sensation of difficult breathing. Terry stated that she needed to balance the energy and he would be all right. She proceeded to transmit energy to his lungs and Jim felt he could breathe normally again. When Terry's hands were over Jim's feet, he felt pulsating energy radiating up his legs. After the healing he felt very relaxed, very good and somewhat healthy again. The abdominal pain had markedly improved, but the most extraordinary improvement was that Jim was able to eat again. Jim had not eaten for nearly a week, because every time he ate he developed severe abdominal pain. After the healing, however, he began eating like a horse. For nearly one hour, Jim ate and ate and ate. He was eating so much that his mother felt he would become severely ill, but to their surprise he did not get sick. He felt fine.

Two weeks after the healing, Jim returned to the doctor's office and his appearance had markedly improved. Even more remarkable was that his liver enzyme levels had returned to near normal, and his doctor was in a state of disbelief. His doctor stated that he had never seen anything like it and asked Jim if he had done anything special. Jim hesitated, and then mentioned that he had seen a healer. The doctor looked at Jim again in disbelief and then said, "Well, whatever you did, keep it up." Jim saw Terry one more time and two weeks later his liver enzyme levels were normal.

Besides feeling physically back to normal, Jim felt more serene, more at ease and relaxed. This seems to be a common feeling among those who have been healed.

CHAPTER TEN
ANXIETY DISORDER

Tony was a macho "Italian Stallion," at least on the outside. He was the boss of his household, the boss over his wife, and had the outward appearance of being in control of his environment and those around him. Underneath things were quite different. Tony was plagued by fears, anxiety and insecurity. Many of Tony's fears and anxieties stemmed from childhood.

Tony experienced his first anxiety attack (panic attack) while taking an exam in school. He described the attack as his heart pounding into his throat, feeling a loss of control, and being so flustered he could no longer think clearly. Thoughts would whirl around, but there was no continuity. The anxiety attacks continued, becoming more frequent, and eventually occurring once a week. The mounting stress at work was the fuel that perpetuated further anxiety and fears.

Eventually, Tony developed a fear of driving, sometimes having anxiety attacks while driving. The fear, as Tony describes it, was a "fear of being too far from home." He would not take any jobs in his profession that were not in close proximity to his home.

In addition to being plagued by anxiety and fears, Tony described himself as extremely negative, suspicious, and unhappy with himself. He finally saw a psychologist who helped him, however, he was still not well, not healed.

Tony's wife had seen Terry and had been helped by her. It was Tony's wife who recommended that he see Terry. Tony was extremely negative, suspicious and felt that this was something akin to the Moonies or even possibly satanic. He wanted nothing to do with it.

Even with the resistance, Tony went to meet Terry, but declined to have a healing. He and his wife talked to Terry for awhile and then his wife had a healing. However, Terry had been praying for Tony during that first meeting, and again before Tony's second meeting.

The second time Tony went to Terry he was again plagued by anxiety. He was nervous, fidgeting and was breaking out in a cold sweat. He was fearful of Terry and suspicious. His healing with her was certainly not a quick fix or an overnight cure. He tossed and fidgeted throughout the entire session, and to be honest, Tony did not feel much different after the session was over. However, with his wife's love and support, Tony continued to see Terry.

Unlike other people who have seen Terry, the healing or the cure did not take two or three sessions. It took a full year. It was five or six healing sessions before Tony even felt there was hope, or began to see light at the end of the tunnel. Tony began to open up, and began to see himself as he truly was inside his thick macho "Italian Stallion" shell; the shell that was shielding the vulnerable, insecure Tony.

In addition to the healings Terry recommended meditation, which Tony had learned before he met Terry. With the help of meditation, Tony's will to get well and the healing sessions, Tony began to clear up the mental discord that were the roots of his fears and anxieties.

During one of Tony's sessions, Terry said that Christ was present. Tony felt like he was floating, and afterwards Terry told him that he had an out of body experience. After the healing he was shaking, crying and overwhelmed.

Today Tony has a healthy mental attitude and an optimistic outlook on life. He feels that life is what you make of it. What you put into it is what you get out of it. He's no longer plagued by fears or anxiety attacks. He no longer has the fear of driving or being too far from home. The macho facade is gone and in its place is an open, warm, friendly, beautiful soul. A striking quality of Tony is his calmness. He's relaxed and peaceful, and as a result performs much better at work. He's happier and has become a very spiritual person. Tony gives, by far, most of the credit for his cure to Terry.

CHAPTER ELEVEN
CHRONIC INFECTIONS and RHEUMATOID DISEASE

Barbara had a great deal of responsibility and stress at work. She became very fatigued and developed swollen lymph glands. A physician prescribed antibiotics, but she remained fatigued and ill. Her friends prompted her to see another physician after an aerobics class, where minor exertion made her totally physically exhausted. The physician thought she had mononucleosis and indeed blood tests confirmed this. He prescribed rest and leaving work until she was better. She was out of work for three and a half weeks, and did feel much better. However, she then returned to the same stressful work environment. Five months later, Barbara had a relapse of mononucleosis. This time she was out of work for five weeks.

Barbara regained her health, but slowly her immune system succumbed to the years of stress. She developed a sinus infection that despite treatment would repeatedly flare up. Two months later she had to totally quit work.

Over the next four years, Barbara was treated for chronic recurrent infections. Sore throats, sinus infections, pneumonias and colds became a recurrent theme in her life. She also developed intense pain in her joints and muscles, from her head to her toes. When examined by her physician, she stated that "I was about to fly through the wall" because the pain was so excruciating. Her doctor diagnosed her as having fibromyalgia. Fibromyalgia is a disease characterized by pain and stiffness in the muscles and joints. Two years later her doctor recommended that she see two to three more doctors. Barbara had never gone through anything as hard as this and she turned to Terry for help.

Barbara was anxious before the first healing with Terry and didn't know what to expect. During the healing she also experienced the heat radiating from Terry's hands. After the healing, she had a haziness in her eyes which persisted for one to two hours, and a sense of calm that she had not experienced at any time in her life. During another healing Barbara had a vision and Terry left her alone in the room. She saw people she had been associated with in her life in front of her in the clouds. Some of these people were dead and some still living.

Barbara credits the turning point in her recovery to when she started receiving treatments from Terry. She continues to see Terry every two to three weeks and has had only a few infections since then. The pain associated with the fibromyalgia has been greatly reduced and there is a 50% improvement in her ability to exercise.

Although Barbara credits the turning point in her health to Terry's healings, she did not say that Terry had helped more than the others taking care of her. She feels that it is a combined effort of a loving husband, concerned physicians and Terry that is winning the battle for her health.

Barbara feels that she is not home free and is only 50% of the way back to a state of good health. However, the severe stress is gone. She is much calmer and has a sense that the battle is being won. Although she did not have a miraculous overnight cure, she is slowly and surely developing good health.

CHAPTER TWELVE
PELVIC PAIN

When Louise Johnson began having pelvic pain, she contacted her gynecologist for evaluation. The pelvic pain was associated with swelling in the lower left part of her abdomen. Louise had a colonoscopy, which enabled her doctor to take a look inside her intestines through a flexible scope. She had other tests, but her doctor was unable to find the cause of her pelvic pain. Louise's gynecologist (doctor who treats women) recommended surgery under general anesthesia. Possibly only minor surgery, with a small incision in her belly button to insert a scope, enabling her gynecologist to see inside her abdomen. However, she might also need a major abdominal surgery.

Louise had a very unpleasant experience with a prior surgery and did not want to have it again! She contacted Terry. Before the first healing Louise did not experience anxiety or apprehension like many others do. When she walked into Terry's home, she felt comfortable, even peaceful. During the first healing she felt intense HEAT radiate from Terry's hands, and a powerful energy surged throughout her entire body. She felt the energy more in certain parts of her body. For instance, she felt an intense energy by her shoulder where she commonly had pain from a condition called intercostal neuralgia. Terry explained that the healing energy would go to the areas most in need of healing.

After the healing Louise felt bouncy, light, exuberant. "It felt like I had just won the Lottery. It was such an incredible feeling, such an incredible high. It was like I could handle anything!" Louise radiated happiness, peace and optimism. Since the first healing Louise has had no further pain in her shoulder. Louise continues to see Terry weekly.

Terry used to be a registered nurse, and is usually very insistent that her clients continue to seek medical attention. Atypically, Terry told Louise that she didn't think surgery was necessary. After three months the pelvic pain and swelling were gone, and neither have recurred in the past two and half years.

Louise also had recurrent genital yeast infections, since she was seventeen years old until 1982. Her gynecologist prescribed Nystatin. This helped, but the yeast infections would recur when she stopped the medication. From 1983 until 1988 she took the Nystatin or other anti-yeast medications, because whenever she stopped the medication the infection recurred. In 1989, one year after initially seeing Terry, Louise stopped the Nystatin and genital yeast infections have not recurred.

One night Louise developed an annoying tension headache. She called Terry to see if there was anything that she could do. Terry told Louise that she could take care of the problem over the phone. Terry instructed Louise to put her hands in water and concentrate on draining the headache into the water. The headache was immediately gone.

Louise is a credit manager and has a great deal of stress from work. Many times she would complain of heaviness in her chest and tension headaches. However, by far the most stress in her life was having a son addicted to cocaine and other drugs, which she never thought possible. Anyway, the healings worked wonders on the stress. She describes herself as a much calmer person, no longer a "screamer." She handles her day to day life much better, and feels like she's much more in control. She does not get the heaviness in her chest anymore, and gets headaches much less frequently. Louise feels that without Terry she would have "flipped out" and couldn't have made it. She continues to see Terry every few months for stress reduction.

CHAPTER THIRTEEN
AIDS

It should be noted that the last two case studies I'm presenting (AIDS and schizophrenia) were not researched by me. I did not interview them nor did I review their medical records, because Terry did not have their addresses, telephone numbers or any way to get in touch with them. Hence, these stories that were told to me by Terry could not be validated by me. I can say that I have never known Terry to lie, for lying is something quite alien to her. With this in mind, I will write about the experience that Terry had with these two patients.

Lenny was young and gay. He had been repeatedly hospitalized for pneumonia with the diagnosis of AIDS. He called Terry not looking for a cure of AIDS, but because he needed to overcome the fear of dying. Lenny came to see Terry with his male lover. According to Terry, Lenny had tested positive for AIDS (HIV

51

positive) and his lover had tested negative for AIDS. HIV is a laboratory test used to confirm a diagnosis of AIDS; HIV positive means that you have the virus that causes AIDS. Lenny and his lover were either abstaining from sex or practicing "safe sex." Lenny was totally passive and submissive before the first healing. During a conversation before the healing, he would frequently turn to his lover for his opinion and asked him if it was OK to have the healing with Terry. Lenny even had to ask his mother before seeing Terry.

Lenny was emaciated, and looked like skin and bones. He had lost considerable weight since his diagnosis of AIDS, and was having severe stomach problems. According to Terry, he looked like he was on his death bed. Lenny knew he was going to die and his only hope was to overcome his fear of dying. Terry tried to get through to him that there is always hope. Terry can tell when a healing is effective by what happens during the healing. "The whole air in the room becomes altered, things become a little blurry rather than hard and distinct. There is no resistance. Your hands move through the air without meeting the sensation of air, and you don't feel the touch of skin when you touch someone. It's as if your hands can move right through the physical body. It's like passing your hand through a wall with no resistance, instead of feeling its hard texture."

Lenny returned for a second healing 6 weeks later. Terry literally did not recognize him. The only way she knew this was Lenny was because he brought his lover with him. He no longer looked hopeless and was more positive. By the third healing Lenny's personality had changed. He was no longer passive and submissive, he had become assertive. Lenny returned to his physician who repeated the AIDS test. This time the test came back HIV negative. This meant that Lenny no longer had the AIDS virus. According to the physician the prior laboratory test must have been in error. Lenny returned to Terry for two more healings. He not only looked well, but he was now aggressive and argued with his lover. Lenny was moving out west with his family, but before leaving he vowed to return to Terry's home with a busload of AIDS patients. Terry simply replied no. She would not turn her home and profession into a circus. If he returned with a busload of AIDS patients she would move. Other AIDS patients have seen Terry with improvement of their disease, and as yet no busload of patients has arrived in her driveway.

CHAPTER FOURTEEN
SCHIZOPHRENIA

George was diagnosed as having schizophrenia and had received extensive treatment throughout his life. He had been treated with many medications and received numerous "shock treatments" (electroconvulsive therapy) over the course of his disease. Surprisingly, he was not on any medication when he first saw Terry.

George was six feet two inches tall and had a large build. When he came to see Terry, the most striking feature was the blank expression on his face and the monotonous tone of his voice. As soon as he entered Terry's home he said, "Well what do you want me to do?" Terry did not feel that a conversation would be as productive as the healing itself and took George directly upstairs for a healing. Terry asked George to lie down on her bed for the healing. He refused because he thought that Terry would give him a shock treatment. They both sat on the bed, and after a matter of minutes Terry had convinced George that she did not have a "shock machine" and he would not be getting a shock treatment. During the healing there was a profound odor in the air, like sulfur or something decaying. George broke out in a profuse sweat and there was again a terrible odor.

By the time of George's second appointment with Terry, he had remarkably improved. He felt much better, and told Terry over the phone he didn't need a second healing. His voice sounded much better, but Terry was insistant that he continue to see his psychiatrist. In fact, she would not end the conversation until he promised to return to his psychiatrist.

Several weeks later George called Terry again and told her that he had seen his psychiatrist. The psychiatrist said there was remarkable improvement and he didn't need to see him until next year. George called Terry one year later to tell her he was still doing well without medication.

CHAPTER FIFTEEN
THEORY BEHIND
THE HEALING POWER

I believe there is a scientific basis behind the healing power, and in the not too distant future it will be discovered. It should first be noted that those who have been given the gift of healing do not heal; we heal ourselves. That is why there is so much interest in the mind-body connection. All human beings have within themselves the ability to cure themselves of any disease, if they had the faith. However, the overwhelming majority of human beings have lost faith and have lost touch with the source. Although Bernie Siegel, Deepak Chopra and others are correct when they state the mind can heal the body, it is most times too much to overcome cancer by positive thinking or a change in attitude. People need to hook up to the source. If they do not have the faith to hook up to the source (i.e. God or higher power) then they need a medium that can do it for them. The healer is simply the medium whereby the individual hooks up to God. The point to be emphasized again is that we heal ourselves via the energy from God.

The healer can be thought of as a catalyst in a chemistry experiment. Two elements alone will react far too slowly in making a compound. However, in the presence of a catalyst the two elements react to form a compound sometimes thousands of times quicker. In this example, the two elements are the individual and the higher power, and the catalyst is the healer. Alone the transformation may be so small as to be unnoticable, but in the presence of a healer (catalyst), the transformation is much quicker.

The classic analogy of the role of the healer is that of an electric fan. The fan has all the properties and parts necessary to blow air, but until the fan is hooked up to the energy source, the fan will not blow air. The fan is the individual to be healed, the cord and the plug are the healer, and the energy source is the higher power (God). We all have the ability to cure ourselves of any disease, if we have sufficient faith. But since most of us do not have sufficient faith, we need someone who can hook us up to the source.

Those who can heal have described an energy which surrounds us and can filter through us. <u>Doctrine and Covenants</u> tells us that "All spirit is matter, but it is more fine or pure, and can only be discerned by purer eyes; We cannot see it; but when our bodies are purified we shall see that it is all matter." Like all matter in the universe, matter is basically energy. A high vibrational energy of such a high frequency that it is as of yet undiscovered. This energy is how God exerts his will upon this earth. Along with the discovery of the atom and DNA, the discovery of this energy (matter) will be the next major scientific breakthrough.

The medium or healer is a focal point that links up this earth which is on the third dimensional plane to the higher dimensions. It is God, the higher power, that exists in the higher dimensions. The focal point is literally connecting the third dimension to higher dimensions. The healer becomes the connecting point between God and the person who needs to be healed. The healer receives the high vibrational energy through the chakras, which are vortexes of whirling energy within our Human Energy Field. Most of the energy enters through the top of the head and the left hand. The healer emits the energy mainly through the heart, hands and eyes. The healer (medium) is actually a transmitter, who transmits the high vibrational energy from God to the person being healed.

This high vibrational energy is transmitted to the human energy field, which actually consists of bodies. Support that these bodies exist is found in the Doctrine and Covenants. Joseph Smith, founder of the Mormon church, describes two bodies called the terrestrial and celestial bodies. Each of these bodies correspond to a different kingdom or degree of glory. The Doctrine and Covenants also states "there are many kingdoms," implying to me that there are many bodies. In eastern religion these kingdoms are called consciousness. These bodies are actually energies of consciousness. The Seik religion teaches that there are ten bodies that all of us have. There are many religious people and many healers who can see many of these bodies.

Barbara Brennan, an extraordinary healer and author of the book Hands of Light, can see many of these bodies and the illustrations of these bodies are from her book. The etheric body (see Figure 1, page 65) is almost a duplicate of the physical body and is linked to the physical body. However, the physical body is composed of atoms and the etheric body is composed of high vibrational energy. Next is the emotional body (see Figure 2, page 66) and it is linked to our emotions. Next is the mental body (see Figure 3, page 67) and it is linked to our cognitive mind and the left hemisphere of the brain. The cognitive mind deals with our speaking, writing, calculations and logic. The next four bodies (astral body, etheric template, celestial body, ketheric template) are linked to our spirit. The astral body (see Figure 4, page 68) is a link between our physical body and our spirit. The etheric template (higher physical body, see Figure 5, page 69) is a spiritual overlay of our physical body. The celestial body (higher emotional body, see Figure 6, page 70) is linked to our higher emotions, for example, unconditional love. The ketheric template (causal body, higher mental body, see Figure 7, page 71) is linked to our intuitive mind and the right hemisphere of the brain. Our intuitive mind deals with our free, spontaneous, non-linear thinking and is responsible for inspiration, creativity and direct cognition (direct knowing, inner knowing). The human aura (human energy field) (see Figure 12, page 75) is a composite (summation) of our high vibrational energy bodies (see Figure 10, page 73).

The high vibrational energy is transmitted through the healer to the bodies of high vibrational energy surrounding our physical body. Just as electromagnetic radiation exists on a continuous spectrum of vibrational frequencies (see Figure 8, page 72), so does the high vibrational energy (see Figure 9, page 72).

The healer does not transmit the whole spectrum of these high vibrational energies equally; instead the healer transmits mainly those frequencies needed for the disease or illness the person has. As seen in figure 9 (page 72), the lowest frequencies of the high vibrational energy correspond to the etheric body. There are certain frequencies within the etheric body range that are used for different diseases of the physical body. For instance, the lowest frequencies are used on bone, to cure such diseases as arthritis. Frequencies a little higher than this are used on tendons as in tendonitis. Frequencies a little higher than this are used on cancer. The highest frequencies in the etheric body range are used on tissues of watery consistency, for example urine. Next on the spectrum of high vibrational energy is the emotional body. Emotional problems such as hatred, resentment, and envy are cured by the lowest frequencies in the emotional body range. Frequencies a little higher than this are used for long standing phobias and frequencies higher than this are used for acute fear. The highest frequencies in the emotional body range are used for emotions like grief. Next on the spectrum of high vibrational energies are those used for dealing with diseases of the spirit. The highest and most subtle of the high vibrational energies are involved with spiritual awakening.

The entry point for the high vibrational energy into these bodies is what is called chakras. They are vortexes of whirling energy within each of these bodies and the entry and exit points for the vibrational energy. To let the high vibrational energy into the body the corresponding chakra rotates clockwise. To let energy out of the body, the corresponding chakra rotates counterclockwise. Hence, we are not a closed system with only a physical body; rather we are an "open system" linked to the universe by our human energy fields which are constantly in flux with the high vibrational energies.

As stated above, different frequencies on the spectrum of high vibrational energy correspond to each of the high vibrational energy bodies, as illustrated in figure 9 (page 72). As in quantum mechanics or atomic theory, there are quantum leaps by the electron when a certain energy level is reached. In atomic theory the atom is made up of a nucleus of protons and neutrons and the electrons rotate in orbit around the nucleus, in a manner similiar to how the planets rotate around the sun. When the electrons reach a certain amount of energy, they jump from their current energy level to the next energy level, which is called a quantum leap.

Quantum mechanics is consistent with atomic theory in many aspects, for instance the quantum leap by electrons to the next energy level. Quantum mechanics states that we do not know the path of the electron as it travels around or about the nucleus. All we can do is predict where we can find the electron most of the time. Furthermore, the electron that is in motion around the nucleus may be very close to the nucleus or an enormously large distance away from the nucleus.

The high vibrational energy that surrounds all of us behaves in an amazingly similiar manner. For example, all the high vibrational energies below a certain frequency correspond to the etheric body. However, at a certain vibrational frequency there is a quantum leap to the next energy level (see Figure 9, page 72), which corresponds to the next body, which in this case would be the emotional body. Increasing in frequency along the high vibrational energy scale, the high vibrational energies correspond to the emotional body until a certain vibrational frequency is achieved and then there is a quantum leap to the mental body level.

The high vibrational energy bodies that surround our physical body are not limited to where the outline of the bodies are seen. The drawings of the bodies simply illustrate where you can find the energy most of the time. Analoguous to quantum mechanics where the electron can be found an enormously large distance away from the nucleus, so can the high vibrational energy be found an enormously large distance away from our physical body. In other words, our high vibrational energy bodies can extend out very large distances from our physical body. This helps explain reports of one identical twin feeling pain when the other identical twin is hurt hundreds of miles away. Although the physical bodies of the twins are separate their human energy fields are linked. This model also helps explain a great deal of spiritual and psychic phenomena.

The influx of this high vibrational energy into the person who is being healed brings about an altered state, described by the person being healed as euphoric and peaceful. Some describe the altered state as floating, being disconnected with their body (feeling outside their body). Most describe the experience as a state of extreme relaxation, very similiar to the state achieved by deep hypnosis. It is not just the mental state of the person being healed that changes. The human energy field and the physical body also change. Terry can tell when a healing is working, because she feels the consistency of the body of the person she's healing change. Instead of feeling bone and muscle as we feel our own body, Terry feels the consistency of the body is more like air.

Another principle of modern physics states that everything in the universe has both mass and waveform properties. Henceforth, our bodies, tables, and cars which are considered to be mass, also exist as a waveform. Light and radio waves, which are primarily thought of as waves of energy, also have mass. Although the bodies that surround all of us are made up of waves of energy, this energy also has mass. Just as those who have spiritual eyes can see these bodies, those with spiritual feelings can actually feel these bodies. They can feel these bodies because these bodies have mass, as well as waveform properties.

In the altered state the physical body can literally change. There are numerous reports of people with shortened legs, arms or fingers, having them lengthen in church where the whole congregation has seen it. There is no principle or law in modern science that accounts for miraculous changes in the physical body that occur during healing. However, if we apply the laws and principles of modern physics to healing, then these miraculous changes are not so difficult to understand.

First, the universe and EVERYTHING in the universe is basically energy. This includes man, plants, animals, water, light, heat, electricity, and so forth. Next, everything in this universe is in a state of flux. One form of energy is constantly being transformed into another form of energy. Light is transformed into heat, heat is transformed into electricity, electricity puts vehicles in motion, which is also energy. The body that you think is so permanent and unchanging is in a state of constant transformation. Your body is made of atoms and these atoms consist of electrons, protons and neutrons. These electrons, protons and neutrons are made up of subatomic particles, that are in a constant state of transformation. When these subatomic particles collide, they produce other subatomic particles which emit light and are transformed into other subatomic particles. Light combines with one subatomic particle to produce an entirely different subatomic particle. Thus, our bodies are in a constant state of flux, where one type of energy is being transformed into another type of energy.

Next, is the law of the Conservation of Energy. This law of physics states energy can neither be created nor destroyed, however, energy can be transformed into another type of energy. This means that when electricity is transformed into heat for making toast, that energy is not lost, it is only transformed. Furthermore, high vibrational energy is also energy. This energy is also in a state of transformation with the other energies (heat, light, atoms, electricity, etc.). Atoms, which make up our body, can be transformed into high vibrational energy and high vibrational energy can be transformed into atoms. Therefore, when a tumor miraculously disappears during a healing, the atoms of the tumor were transformed into high vibrational energy and removed from the body. When a finger grows back in a matter of seconds, it is high vibrational energy that is being transformed into atoms of the finger. Here, the high vibrational energy creates the etheric body of the finger, which is the template (blue print) for the finger. Then high vibrational energy is transformed into the atoms which make up the new finger.

When the etheric body is changed, the physical body

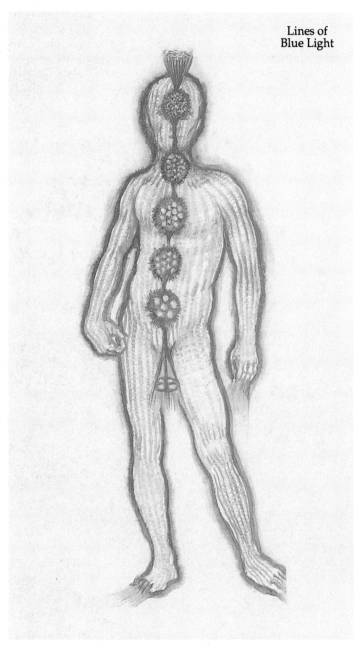

Lines of
Blue Light

Figure 1 - The Etheric Body

65

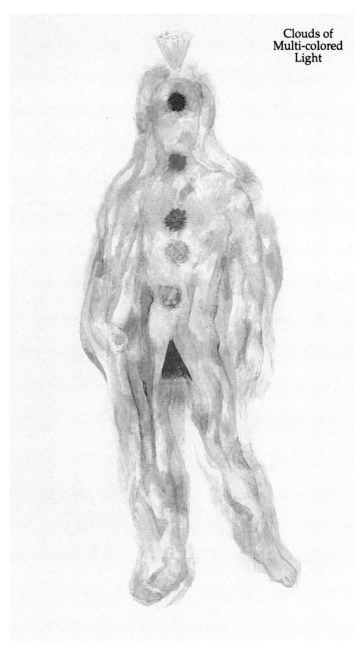

Clouds of
Multi-colored
Light

Figure 2 - The Emotional Body

66

Lines of
Yellow Light

Figure 3 - The Mental Body

67

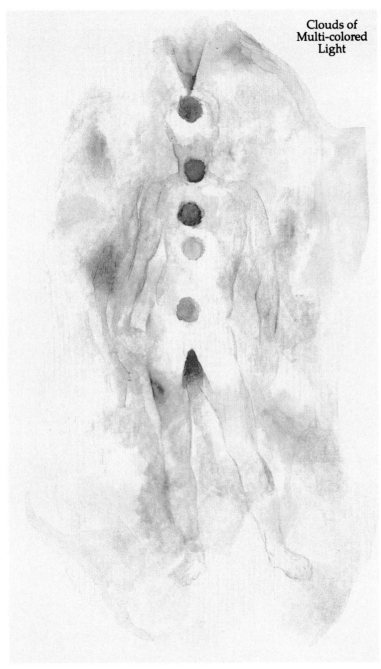

Clouds of
Multi-colored
Light

Figure 4 - The Astral Body
68

Figure 5 - The Etheric Template Level

69

Figure 6 - The Celestial Body

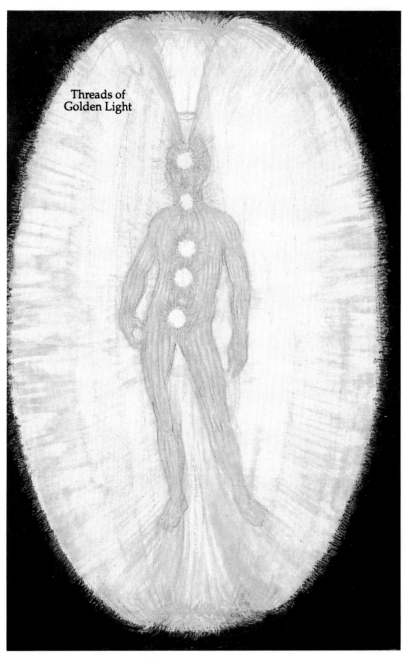

Threads of
Golden Light

Figure 7 -The Ketheric Template Level

71

COMPARISON OF ELECTROMAGNETIC ENERGY SPECTRUM
VS.
HIGH VIBRATIONAL ENERGY SPECTRUM

HIGH VIBRATIONAL ENERGY SPECTRUM
ELECTROMAGNETIC ENERGY SPECTRUM

Frequency Hz	Wavelength m	Nomenclature	Typical Source
10^{23}	3×10^{-15}	Cosmic Photons	Astronomical
10^{22} - 10^{20}	3×10^{-14} - 3×10^{-12}	X-rays	Radioactive Nucleus
10^{18} - 10^{16}	3×10^{-10} - 3×10^{-8}	Ultraviolet	Atoms in Sparks
10^{15}	3×10^{-7}	Visible Light	Atoms, Molecules
10^{14} - 10^{12}	3×10^{-6} - 3×10^{-4}	Infrared	Hot Bodies
10^{11} - 10^{10}	3×10^{-3} - 3×10^{-2}	Microwaves	Electronic Devices
10^9	.3	Radar	Electronic Devices
10^8	3	Television	Electronic Devices
10^7 - 10^5	30 - 3000	Radio	Electronic Devices
100 - 10	3×10 - 3×10	Power	Rotating Machinery
0	Infinity	Direct Current	Batteries

Figure 8

HIGH VIBRATIONAL ENERGY SPECTRUM

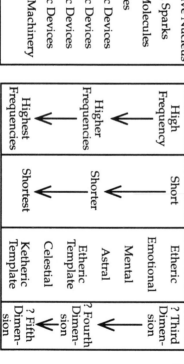

Frequency Hz	Wavelength m	Body	Source
High Frequency	Short	Etheric	? Third Dimension
←	←	Emotional	←
Higher Frequencies	Shorter	Astral	? Fourth Dimension
←	←	Mental	←
		Etheric Template	
Highest Frequencies	Shortest	Celestial	? Fifth Dimension
←	←	Ketheric Template	←

Figure 9

72

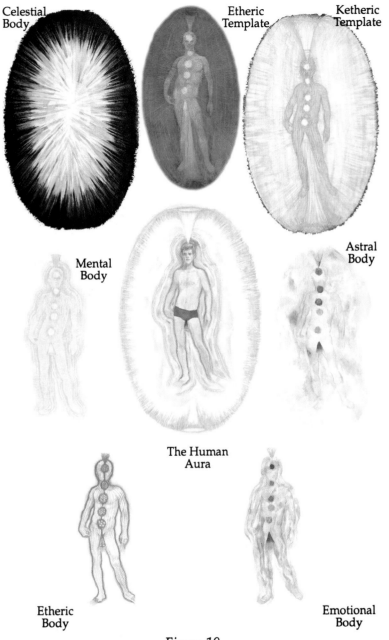

Celestial
Body

Etheric
Template

Ketheric
Template

Mental
Body

Astral
Body

The Human
Aura

Etheric
Body

Emotional
Body

Figure 10
THE HUMAN AURA (HUMAN ENERGY FIELD)
is the composite of our high vibrational energy bodies.

73

Figure 11

Seven Layers Visible

Figure 12
The Human Aura
(Human Energy Field)

75

Figure 13

Our Lady of Guadalupe

Figure 14

Our Lady of Refugio

Figure 15
St. Joseph

Figure 16
Jesus
(copyright 1982 Marians of the Immaculate Conception)

Figure 17

will also be changed, because they are linked to each other. The etheric body is the blueprint of the physical body, but is made up of high vibrational energy. When the emotional body is changed, our emotional makeup will also be changed. The same principle applies to the rest of the bodies. While in this altered state, it is the individual's spirit or true essence that heals the body, mind and spirit. The spirit heals the body, mind and spirit with the specific frequencies of high vibrational energy needed for the specific disease to be healed. Here healing implies a persistent change of the body, mind and spirit toward the state of health. Any disease can be cured, any ailment can be overcome.

Healers can diagnose disease by analyzing the human energy field and treat disease by changing the human energy field. Many healers can see or feel changes in the human energy field corresponding to diseases of the body, mind or spirit.

Although cancer is cured at the physical level, that is not the only area where the healer works. Many qualified healers believe that there is also disease at other levels that may be causing the physical disease. For instance, certain emotional problems and mental attitudes may create such distress that they cause a breakdown in our immune system, making us susceptible to cancer. It is very important to cure these emotional problems and mental attitudes. They can again lead to distress and breakdown in our immune system, making the person vulnerable to a recurrence of the cancer.

Stress plays a key role in the development of physical and mental illness. Many illnesses start at the spiritual level and these illnesses could be prevented if the spiritual energy fields were in tune. Imbalance at the spiritual level causes stress and eventually distress. This distress at the spiritual level leads to spiritual sickness. Spiritual distress leads to mental stress, then eventually mental distress and mental illness. This mental illness may be emotional, attitudinal, sexual, interpersonal or even depressive. It is this mental illness and mental distress that leads to physical stress and eventually physical distress and physical illness. Mental distress and illness causes a breakdown of our normally well-functioning psychoneuroimmunology, which makes us susceptible to physical disease.

In medical school my colleagues who wanted to go into psychiatry were sometimes annoyed that they had to learn so much about the body, when all they were interested in was the mind. They strongly felt that the mind and the body were separate and had nothing to do with each other. However, as they progessed in their psychiatric training, my colleagues were impressed by the connection of the mind and the body. They saw how diseases of the mind can effect the body and how diseases of the body can effect the mind. The same is true with the spirit. The body, mind and spirit are all interconnected and diseases of one can effect the other two. As stated above, many diseases start at the spiritual level and it is disease of the spirit which can cause disease of the mind, which in turn can cause disease of the body.

Terry does a great deal of her healing at the spiritual level, and it was this part of her work that was left out of this book. Terry and I felt that we would lose the focus of this book if I included this part of her work. Those people who are spiritually developed and spiritually healthy are much more easily healed than those individuals who are not spiritually developed or

healthy. For example, a very loving and giving human-
itarian would be more easily healed than a lying,
cheating murderer. Terry can feel the difference when
performing healings. She says that healing a human-
itarian or someone who is spiritually developed is like
breaking through soft plastic. When she tries healing
individuals who are not spiritually developed or who
are spiritually sick, it's like trying to break through
concrete.

Very important in healing is balancing the subtle
energies (high vibrational energies) and letting the
energy flow freely throughout the human energy field.
You may have a beautifully engineered car but if one of
the parts of the car is functioning poorly, it can make a
significant difference in the performance of the car.
Furthermore, you may have the finest parts of all the
best cars in the world, but if they don't fit together and
work well together, your car may not work. The same
is true with our human energy field. All the energies
must be balanced, flowing fluently, and everything
integrated in order for us to feel at our best and
perform at our best.

A final point to be made is that the priest who has
been given the power of healing does not consciously
think of what energies are needed for the healing to
take place. There is a subliminal connection between
the spirits of the healer, the person being healed and
God. The spirit knows which energy frequencies are
needed and it becomes an automatic superconscious
process.

CHAPTER SIXTEEN
RESEARCH

There have been many articles and books written about the gift of healing by the laying on of hands. There have also been many case studies done about miraculous cures. What is needed now is research and controlled scientific experiments. It is only through controlled scientific studies that we will prove or disprove the healing power. It is through science that we will learn the scientific basis for the healing power. What is absolutely not needed is political debates between the believers and the nonbelievers, whereby nothing is accompished except political objectives. The ultimate truth as to whether the healing power exists or not will be found through science.

I have provided 14 case studies which document what appears to be healing by the laying on of hands. And I will outline in this chapter many case studies by other authors who have documented what appears to

84

be the healing by the laying on of hands. However, case studies are not proof that the healing power exists. What is needed is controlled scientific experiments and statistical analysis. In this chapter I will discuss many case studies and controlled scientific studies giving credibility to the healing power.

In the Journal of Perspectives in Biology and Medicine the authors Richard and Enid Peschel give three case studies whereby the patients had terminal cancer and were cured by medical therapy and prayers. T.C. Everson (and group) has published 130 documented cases of spontaneous regression of cancer in the journals which include the Annals of Surgery. What is not known in all of these documented cases is how much faith and the healing power helped in the cure of the cancer. It is well known that the body can at times produce antibodies to kill off cancer cells and this may be taking place without the help of the healing power.

In the Journal of Family Practice, the authors King, Sobal and DeForge reported a cross-sectional survey administered to 207 family practice patients. Results showed that "58% of the patients felt that faith healers are quacks, 29% believed that faith healers can help some people whom physicians cannot help, 34% stated that faith healers and physicians can work together, 21% had attended faith healing service, 6% stated they had been healed by faith healers and 15% reported they personally knew someone who had been healed." It is Terry's and my shared belief that a significant percentage of the healing profession are fakes or unqualified, therefore it is easier to understand why so many people don't believe in faith healing. If all faith healers had Terry's gift, I believe the results of this study would be altered dramatically in support of faith healers. What does make an impression on me after reading this study is that 34% of those surveyed felt that physicians and faith healers can work together.

A questionnaire study from the Netherlands on over 3,000 patients who saw sixty different healers showed that approximately "two thirds of the patients showed definite improvement." Three other studies have shown similiar success rates for healing (Haraldsson and Olafsson, Turner, Geddes). One other study by Finkler showed a 25% success rate for patients who went to a "spiritist" temple in Mexico.

Lourdes is a "power spot," a place where the healing energy abounds and miracles are known to occur. People come from around the world to seek cures for various diseases and ailments. Cases that are believed to be miracles are examined closely by the Lourdes Medical Bureau and then reexamined by the Association of Lourdes Doctors and the International Medical Commission. As of 1954, the Lourdes Medical Bureau had "upheld" 1,200 cures in people who had made the pilgrimage to Lourdes. Theologians, however, have much stricter criteria before they call something a miracle. Of the 1,200 cases reported to be cured by the Lourdes Medical Bureau, only forty nine met all the criteria to be "proclaimed miraculous by the theologians."

CASE STUDIES

There are hundreds of case studies in the literature documenting healing by the laying on of hands. Some are well documented and others are not well documented. Some of these case studies are noteworthy.

A case of a transsexual was published in the Archives of Sexual Behavior. John had considered himself female since childhood. As a teenager John had enlarged breasts, and was cross-living as Judy. Psychological gender identity tests consistently assessed John as female. John made arrangements for a sex change operation. Prior to the scheduled surgery Judy went to another doctor, after persuasion by a friend. The doctor stated that John (Judy) was possessed and the doctor performed an exorcism. After the exorcism, John "threw away Judy's clothes, cut his hair" and identified himself as being a male. Several weeks after the exorcism John was taken to a faith healer. By the end of the healing by the faith healer, John's enlarged (female) breasts had disappeared and have not recurred since. Follow up psychological gender identity tests confirmed male gender for John, and there has been no regression in two years of follow up.

The case of Marolyn Ford was medically well documented and dramatic enough that she wrote a book about it called, These Blind Eyes Now See. After graduating from high school, Marolyn's eyesight began to fail her. An ophthomologist at Mayo Brothers Medical Center in Rochester, Minnesota diagnosed Marolyn as having macular degeneration. This is a disease that effects the central vision, but leaves peripheral vision. Although Marolyn had peripheral vision she was legally blind. Ten years later Marolyn began losing her peripheral vision, and a specialist in ophthomology in Houston, Texas told her that she was going totally blind. At the age of thirty one, Marolyn and her Pastor husband had prayed for years for the Lord to restore her eyesight. One night after reading the <u>Bible</u>, Marolyn's husband began to cry and pray with her. "Oh, God! You can restore Marolyn's eyesight tonight, Lord. I know you can do it! And, God, if it be Your will, I pray You will do it tonight." At that instant her eyesight was restored. News spread quickly of this miracle. The ophthomologist had heard of the miracle before the appointment was made with him. After thorough examination by the doctor, he exclaimed that the disease that effected her eyes was unchanged. The retina (the part of the eye that relays light input enabling us to see) was still "massive scar tissue" and the "optic nerve is dead," according to the report given to Marolyn by the ophthomologist. He told her that she should not be able to see, but she now had 20/25 vision (nearly perfect vision).

An article in <u>American Medical News</u> (a weekly newspaper distributed by the American Medical Association) published January 26, 1990 by Deborah Pinkney is entitled "Native Healers." It is an article about the kahunas of Hawaii. The kahunas are native Hawaiians known to be very powerful healers. There are sixty to eighty kahunas in Hawaii, but only ten are professional healers. Dr Blaisdell, who teaches medicine at the University of Hawaii, is confident that western-trained physicians in Hawaii and the kahunas can work together. In addition, he gave an example of a man with terminal cancer who responded to the kahunas' healings. Other physicians have been similiarly impressed with the cures proclaimed by some kahunas. "There have been some rather miraculous healings occurring with native Hawaiian healing practices," Dr. Shintani said.

There have been books published about extra-ordinary healers like Terry. In the book <u>Born to Heal</u> by Ruth Montgomery, the author describes the life of a very powerful healer. The book gives a detailed account of this extraordinary healer and numerous people interviewed by Ruth Montgomery who were healed by him.

I have investigated two individuals who claimed to be healed of the AIDS virus by God and Christ. I can not prove that they were cured of the AIDS virus by the healing power, but I did confirm the lab results. Both of these individuals were HIV positive then, later, HIV negative. Here HIV positive means the individual has the AIDS virus and will eventually develop AIDS, and HIV negative means that the individual does not have the AIDS virus. Medical doctors rationalize this to laboratory error. Here are the remarkable stories of these individuals who claimed to be cured of AIDS.

Andre Williams wrote a book titled <u>God Heals, Aids Kills/ God Healed Me Of The Aids Virus</u>. Andre had led a life of promiscuity, and was unaware of the risk he was taking. He was a diabetic requiring insulin shots and was prescibed a pain killer by his dentist. The combination of insulin and pain killer put Andre in the emergency room, in a semi-coma and on a respirator. He felt he was going to die and cried for God's help. "I asked him to forgive me of my sins...I told him if He (God) would leave me on this earth, I would put him first in my life." He felt God's embrace and was no longer scared of dying. He was in the intensive care unit for two weeks, but walked out of the hospital. He decided to have a check up and was tested for the HIV virus. A few days later, a nurse gave him the results of the test and told him he tested positive for the AIDS virus. She explained about AIDS and the progression of the disease, then she told him "prepare yourself to die." Andre was shocked, but knew that God could heal him, for "God is still a God of miracles." He lost weight and developed symptoms consistent with AIDS. One day while watching television, Robert Tilton was praying for the sick. He placed his hands on the television and began praying. "I cried out to the Lord and I felt the Holy Spirit touch me and that heavy burden I had been carrying just lifted. I heard the Lord telling me in my spirit "you're all right." I knew I was healed then and there." He had the INNER KNOWING that he would test negative for the AIDS virus. A second test showed indeed he was HIV negative, and no longer had the AIDS virus. He cried when he received the news and "praised the Lord. He (God) told me 'Now go tell the world what I have done for you. I can do the same for them if they come to me as children and ask.' "

Evan is another remarkable story of someone who was diagnosed with AIDS and now no longer has the AIDS virus. He had not been in any high risk group for acquiring the AIDS virus. He and his wife were virgins when they were married and they remained strictly monogamous. In the fall of 1990, he had a stroke and became extremely ill. During the course of his hospitalization he became critically ill and received blood products. While recovering from his stroke and illness, he was overcome with sudden overwhelming fear. "It felt like I was dying." Evan cried out, "Dear Jesus help me!" He could hear Jesus saying, "Don't be afraid, nothing can happen to you that I can not take care of." In January 1991, while still in the hospital, his physicians had discovered an abnormal opening between his lungs and his esophagus that had to be operated on. However, his doctors also found a fungus growing in his throat, commonly found in patients who have AIDS. Two separate blood tests confirmed that he was HIV positive. His doctors told him he would eventually die of AIDS. Evan had surgery for the opening between his lungs and his esophagus and spent another two months recovering in the hospital. His family and his church members had been praying for him while he had been in the hospital, but he can not recall any cataclysmic burst of energy from the healing power. Jesus told Evan "Don't worry about this I can take care of it. Have them test your blood again." When he told his doctors that he wanted to be tested again, they were very concerned that he did not want to face reality. As a matter of fact, his doctors were a little annoyed with him and his inability to face the facts. Evan convinced his doctors that as long as he was paying for it, he should be able to have the HIV blood tests again. Before he received the test results, he remembers an inner peace, and an INNER KNOWING that the test results would come back HIV negative. Five different blood tests for the HIV virus came back HIV negative.

Although case studies are helpful in shining light on the subject of healing, they are not proof that the healing power exists. Only through controlled scientific experiments will we prove or disprove the healing power.

CONTROLLED STUDIES

A well controlled, randomized double-blind study (for a description and significance of a double-blind study see Double-Blind Study in this chapter) was performed to observe the effects of the healing energy on wound healing in mice. These experiments were conducted by the Department of Physiology at the University of Manitoba. Skin was cut off the backs of mice and then the mice were randomly assigned to be given healings by an authentic healer. Medical students were used as control fake healers. The studies showed a statistically significant faster rate of wound healing in the group of mice given healings by the healer.

Several articles have been published showing a "telekinetic effect on plant growth" including experiments performed at Duke University. A book was published called The Power of Prayer on Plants written by Reverend Loehr. This book describes the positive effect of prayer on growth of kernels of corn, lima beans and sweet pea seeds that were watered with water blessed with prayer.

A well controlled randomized double-blind study was performed to observe the effects of healing on the rate of growth of plants. Barley seeds were placed in soil under conditions that were not optimal for plant growth. The seeds were initially watered with 1% salt water and then the soil was dried for several days. Then an authentic healer gave healing energy to water that would be used to water half of the plants in a randomly assigned double-blind fashion. The other half of the plants were watered with water that was not given healing energy. These studies showed a statistically significant greater growth in the plants grown with the water given healing energy by the healer. Several other studies on plant growth by water treated by healers or direct healing have also reported success (Grad, Hickman, Nicholas, Vasse, Loehr, Miller).

Electromagnetic Field

Although I studied magnetism thoroughly while taking physics in college, I did not fully understand it. I have a feeling that I did not fully understand it, because physicists do not fully understand it. There are many aspects of magnetism that have not been completely explained. What is known is that the earth generates an electromagnetic field, which is measurable. What is not well known is that our bodies also generate an electromagnetic field. However, since the mass of the earth is millions of times greater than the mass of our bodies the electromagnetic field we generate by our bodies will be extremely difficult to measure.

During the healings by Terry, there is a strong magnetic field generated around Terry and the person being healed. By the end of the healing session, Terry can feel this strong electromagnetic field. Many scientists are working on measuring this electromagnetic field surrounding all of us.

Terry told me that she could alter what has been put on an audio cassette tape simply by the magnetic field generated by her hands. I knew I could not print this in my book without having performed an experiment to verify this ability of Terry's. Furthermore, being a scientist, I have a healthy amount of skepticism, and a need to verify these miracles through science. I gave Terry a cassette tape on which I had recorded several songs by the group, the Beach Boys. I played the entire cassette back to make sure that the songs had been recorded properly. Terry held the cassette in her hands, while she generated a powerful magnetic field with her hands. I then played the cassette and found that several of the songs on the tape had been partially erased. It sounded as if they had been muffled, while other songs on the cassette had been relatively unchanged. Anyway, this experiment had confirmed what Terry had told me.

If Terry can produce a magnetic field powerful enough to erase a cassette tape then we should be able to measure the electromagnetic field generated by her hands. I should clarify that the electromagnetic field and the high vibrational energy are different. The heat and the electromagnetic field that is generated by the healer's hands is a by-product of the high vibrational energy emitted by the healer's hands.

Kirlian Photography

Some of the most elegant research that now sheds light on the healing power has been in the field of Kirlian photography. Kirlian photography is accomplished by taking an object to be photographed and placing it in a high frequency electrical field over a photographic negative. The pictures are probably the result of an interaction between the high frequency electrical field produced by the voltage generator and the high frequency vibrational energy that surrounds all of us. The Kirlian photographs allow us to indirectly see the high vibrational energy that surrounds all of us.

The high vibrational energy that surrounds human beings, plants and animals is seen by people like Terry as a special light, commonly called the aura. This energy that surrounds our bodies is termed the Human Energy Field and consists of the high vibrational energy that surrounds and permeates all of us. It is the Human Energy Field that the healers work on. When you change the Human Energy Field, you also change

F. F. Strong demonstrating effects of Tesla coil (courtesy, S. Krippner).

Figure 18

FIGURE 25. Electrophotograph, right index finger pad, control "healer" during state of rest. (courtesy, T. Moss).

FIGURE 26. Electrophotograph, right index finger pad, control "healer" following attempted healing. (courtesy, T. Moss).

FIGURE 21. Electrophotograph, right index finger pad, "healer" during state of rest. (courtesy, T. Moss).

FIGURE 22. Electrophotograph, right index finger pad, "healer" following attempted healing. (courtesy, T. Moss).

FIGURE 23. Electrophotograph, right index finger pad, control patient during state of rest. (courtesy, T. Moss).

FIGURE 24. Electrophotograph, right index finger pad, control patient following attempted healing (courtesy, T. Moss).

FIGURE 19. Electrophotograph, right index finger pad, patient during state of rest. (courtesy, T. Moss).

FIGURE 20. Electrophotograph, right index finger pad, patient following "healer's" attempted healing. (courtesy, T. Moss).

FIGURE 27. Electrophotograph, mutilated companula leaf, untreated. (courtesy, T. Moss).

FIGURE 28. Electrophotograph, mutilated companula leaf after treatment. (courtesy, T. Moss).

Correlation Between Human Energy Field and Personal Space

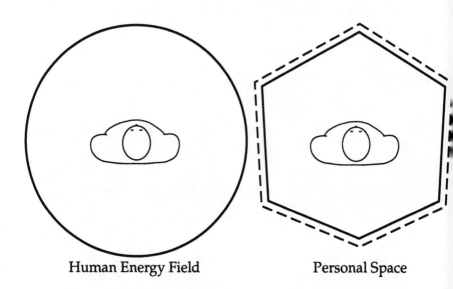

Human Energy Field   Personal Space

(The figure on the left shows the boundaries of the Human Energy Field and the figure on the right shows the boundaries of personal space. The personal space dotted line represents the distance at which a male feels uncomfortable with another male and the solid opposite line represents the distance at which a male feels uncomfortable with a female. Any closer and the male feels uncomfortable, or in other words, the male feels that the male or female is invading his "personal space.")

Figure 29

the physical body, since they are interconnected.

Dramatic evidence that an energy field truly does exist is found when photographing a leaf that was recently broken in two. Although part of the leaf is missing, the light still remains surrounding where the whole leaf used to be (see Figure 11, page 74). A Kirlian photograph taken of Mr. F. Strong (see Figure 18, page 95) shows the energy field surrounding his body.

Controlled experiments have been performed using healers and Kirlian photography. Kirlian photographs were taken of the tip of the index finger of the patient and healer before and after the healing. Results showed an increase in energy surrounding the finger tip of the patient (see Figure 19 and 20, page 96) and a decrease in energy surrounding the finger tip of the healer (see Figure 21 and 22, page 96). This demonstrates a transfer of energy from the healer to the patient. These test results were reproducible. When control experiments were done with a fake healer, who mimicked a healing, there was no significant change in the size of the energy field as seen on the Kirlian phottgraphs (see Figures 23,24,25 and 26, page 96).

Further experiments were done on plants and healers. When a campanula leaf was mutilated by the experimenters they found a decrease in leaf's luminescence (see Figure 27, page 97). When the mutilated leaf was given a healing treatment by a healer there was increased luminescence in the campanula leaf (see Figure 28, page 97).

The Human Energy Field

The Human Energy Field surrounds our bodies and

is egg-shaped as seen in Figure 12 (page 75). There are many holy men and women who can see this egg-shaped field of energy that surrounds each of us. There are many more who can see part of this energy field, which is commonly called the human aura. Some healers can see the Human Energy Field and some can feel it. Terry can see and feel the Human Energy Field. A book by George Ritchie M.D., called <u>Return from Tomorrow</u> gives support that this Human Energy Field actually exists. George Ritchie describes in his book an after life (near death) experience where he is shown our world by Jesus as it looks through spiritual eyes. George Ritchie saw many important aspects of our world from a spirit vantage point, and he saw that we are all surrounded by a "cocoon of light." George Ritchie states in his book that "All of the living people we were watching were surrounded by a faint luminous glow, almost like an electrical field over the surface of their bodies. This luminosity moved as they moved, like a second skin made out of pale, scarcely visible light."

Throughout the <u>Bible</u> are accounts of prophets seeing angels, Jesus Christ and even God the Father. They have seen a very bright light surrounding these heavenly beings and emanating from them. St. John states that "the light (light of Christ) lighteth every man that cometh forth into the world." The more we keep the Commandments of God, the more the light of Christ can shine through us. After Moses spoke to God on Mt. Sinai "the skin of Moses shone."

Many of the world's major religions have drawings and paintings of their saints and holy men, with halos of light surrounding their heads or bodies. (Figure13 on page 76) shows the classic egg-shaped aura (human energy field) surrounding the virgin Mary (Our Lady of Guadalupe). Figure 14 on page 77 shows the aura surrounding Our Lady of Refugio. Figure 15 on page 78 shows the halo of light around the head of St. Joseph. Figure 16 on page 79 shows a halo of light around Jesus and the light of Christ coming from his heart. The reason so many of the Catholic drawings show the light shining around the head of the saints and not the whole body, is because the light around the head is more easily seen with spiritual eyes. The light around the whole body in the form of the egg is more difficult to see.

Further evidence that the Human Energy Field exists comes from studies in psychology and psychiatry. Researchers have concluded that human beings have "personal space" surrounding them. This appears to be an extension of the physical body. Researcher Von Uexkull uses the analogy of "people surrounded by soap-bubble worlds." Experiments were performed with people to see how close they could get to each other before they felt "uncomfortable about closeness." The results of the experiment are shown in figure 29 on page 98. The dotted line represents the mean distance at which a male feels uncomfortable with another male. The solid line represents the mean distance at which a male feel uncomfortable with a female. Any closer and the male feels that the male or female is invading his "personal space." Results from these experiments led researchers to conclude that ALL human beings are surrounded by personal space. Also, personal space was found to have "surprisingly regular contours" and to be equidistant surrounding the physical body. The human energy field correlates well with experiments on personal space.

HUMAN STUDIES

Eleven patients were studied by Hubacher for the effects of healing by a gifted healer. All eleven of the patients were treated by physicians and "had been told that no further improvement could be expected." These patients were sent to a gifted healer for treatments. Two of the patients responded initially but later regressed, however, "six patients showed considerable improvements confirmed by their physicians."

Double-Blind Study

When scientists want to prove something in clinical medicine the last word is usually a double-blind study. This means that there is no chance of bias in the study because neither the people conducting the study nor the patients themselves know who is receiving the real therapy and medications or mimic therapy and medications. A double-blind study published in the Southern Medical Journal in 1988 evaluated the effects of prayer on patients admitted to the San Francisco General Hospital's Coronary Care Unit. Patients admitted to the Coronary Care Unit were randomly selected into two different groups. One group had prayers given for them by Christians outside the hospital, while the other group served as a control group. The group who had prayers given for them had an overall statistically signicant better hospital course when compared to the control group.

Another double-blind study was done to evaluate the effect of distant healing on 96 patients with high blood pressure by eight healers. The study showed "statistically significant improvement in systolic blood pressure."

Therapeutic Touch

Therapeutic touch is used at New York University (N.Y.U.) Medical School and its effects have been researched. Therapeutic touch utilizes the same energy that Terry uses and a similiar technique. The practitioners are nurses who touch only the patient's energy field (Human Energy Field) to revitalize it, never actually touching the patient's body. They first "center themselves" and enter into a meditative state and then with love and compassion in their heart for the patient they let the energy flow through their hands to the patient's energy field. They glide their hands over the patient about 4 to 6 inches above the patient's body. The practitioners feel the radiation of HEAT from their hands. What is interesting is why this practice is allowed in such a conservative and orthodox institution like N.Y.U. Medical School. In any event, this medical school should be congratulated on their progressive research and policies. Although therapeutic touch is a form of healing by the laying on of hands, this term is avoided. N.Y.U. Medical School has classes where they teach therapeutic touch to those who are interested.

Three well controlled randomized studies done at N.Y.U. Medical School have been published showing the benefit of therapeutic touch. A control group using nurses who mimick therapeutic touch was used in each of the three studies to rule out the possibility of a placebo response. The latest is a National Institute of Health study published in the 1990 Pain Journal. The study measured the amount of pain relief medication needed for patients who had undergone surgery. The results showed that patients who had therapeutic touch required less medication than those patients who did not have therapeutic touch. Another study titled "The Effects of Therapeutic Touch on Tension Headaches" published in <u>Nursing Research</u> in 1986 showed the benefit of therapeutic touch in relieving tension headaches. Patients in the therapeutic touch group had twice the average reduction in headache pain, when compared to the control group. A study titled "Therapeutic Touch As Energy Exchange" published in <u>Advances in Nursing Science</u> in 1984 showed the benefit of therapeutic touch in relieving anxiety. The group who recieved therapeutic touch had a significantly greater reduction in anxiety as compared to the mimic therapeutic touch control group.

Future Research

There will be much more research done on the healing power and the amount of research done will grow exponentially. Many breakthroughs will soon be made. When the research is evaluated by the medical and scientific communities as well as the general public, it should be kept in mind that there are certain places on this earth where miracles are more likely to occur and other places where miracles are unlikely to occur. In the spiritual realm there are places on this earth that are considered to be holy ground. Some people call these areas power spots. They are areas where this high vibrational energy abounds. The holier the ground, the more abundant the high vibrational energy will be. There are certain areas on this earth where miracles are believed to occur. When evaluating the research on the healing power, it will be important to know where the research was done. A healing miracle is more likely to occur in a holy temple in the presence of a powerful healer and true believers, than it is in Joe's Bar in downtown Brooklyn. Where the reseasrch is done can dramatically alter the results of the research.

It is important to keep in mind when analyzing research done on healing, the faith of the person to be healed. Two different people may have the same exact disease, very similar backgrounds and physical makeup. However, even in the presence of a powerful healer on holy ground and the willingness of both to be healed, one will be healed and the other will not. This phenomenon is caused by the internal faith of those who are being healed. Since we are ultimately self healed, we are healed according to our own faith. And as of yet, we do not have a faith-ometer that conveniently lets us measure faith.

The breakthrough in the theory of relativity by Albert Einstein was made because Einstein did not try to put the universe in a tidy little box, which other physicists were trying to do. Instead, he said let the universe be. If we are trying to learn the mysteries of the universe, then we should not force it into a box with boundaries limited by our current beliefs, knowledge, and way of thinking. It was only through Albert Einstein's ability to let the universe be as it is, that we now know time is not constant throughout the universe. It varies relative to where you are. Now Einstein's outlandish concept of relativity has been proven. If we are to find the truth about the healing power, it will not only be important to keep an open mind, but we must also broaden our current way of thinking.

CHAPTER SEVENTEEN
CAUTION

In every profession there are imitators, fakes and people who are unqualified for their profession. The medical profession has its share of this problem, however, it has taken steps to minimize it. The healing profession also has this problem. There will always be people who imitate professionals for the purpose of making money. When people hear stories of people being healed by the laying on of hands, there will appear charlatans, who in order to make money, profess to have been given this gift. These charlatans not only steal peoples' money, but also damage the reputation of the healing profession. The healing professionals that I'm talking about include priests, nuns, Holy men, clergy, and all those who practice healing by the laying on of hands. I recommend caution and the use of prayer if you are in need of a healer.

There are also healers who are not charlatans, but have not developed their skills. For analogy I will use the medical profession. Before someone can perform open heart surgery on you, they must go to college, medical school, do internship, residency and then further specialization in open heart surgery. There are priests, nuns, professional healers, clergy, etc. who are just now developing their gift of healing. You can compare them to medical students, interns, residents and board certified physicians. This group as a whole does not do harm and has the potential for doing good. A novice healer who is just starting to develop his gift of healing can be compared to a second year medical student. Just as the medical student is not qualified to perform open heart surgery, the novice healer is not likely to help heal someone with terminal cancer. However, just as the medical student has the ability to become a top notch open heart surgeon, the novice healer has the potential to become an extraordinary healer.

The next group are those who not only have the healing gift but who have developed their skill. This group is in the minority of those who claim to have the healing power, so it's easy to see why there is skepticism among the general population and the medical profession.

There is a potential for harm, however, even among the legitimate healers. The potential for harm comes from those who deny the benefit the medical profession has to offer. The medical profession is based upon science, with drugs and procedures proven effective. Healers who deny this can be doing their clients a great disservice.

Terry has been gifted by the best of both worlds. She was a practicing registered nurse for many years before entering the healing profession. She will not work with a client until they realize that what she does is no substitute for what their doctors are doing for them. Again, I state my belief that the most powerful means of curing disease is by combining modern day medical technology with the healing power.

CHAPTER EIGHTEEN
A FUTURE HEALER

After the remarkable recovery of a patient with AIDS from Terry's healing, he vowed to return with a busload of AIDS patients. Terry told him that he would do no such thing. If her home became flooded with AIDS patients coming on buses, she would move away. There is only so much work that one person can do. I feel that over the next decade many more people will be given the gift of healing.

Mary was diagnosed as having scoliosis (abnormal curvature of the spine) at the tender age of twelve. She was told that to prevent further progression of her scoliosis, she would need to wear a Milwaukee back brace. This device consisted of one metal bar up the front and two metal bars down the back, which fit around her torso from her hips to her chin. She was told that she would have to wear this device until she was eighteen years old and that it could only be taken off for showers. Being a teenager and having to wear this conspicuous contraption, was a heavy weight to bear. Her peers were sometimes very cruel. Then six months later, Mary was put in a sanitarium for tuberculosis. The combination of scoliosis and tuberculosis was devastating. She spent three months in a sanitarium, and when she came out she was never quite the same. She grew up very quickly, and instead of becoming bitter, she grew stronger. She became aware of the delicate balance of life. This experience not only gave her empathy, but was invaluable in preparing her for the work she would some day perform. Her life had dramatically changed. She was no longer concerned about trivial events, and felt that there has to be more to life than what people usually see.

Ever since she was young, Mary had been fascinated with her hands. Her sister often found Mary staring at or captivated by her hands. In church, instead of listening to the minister or looking at the cute boys, she was staring at her hands.

After interviewing Mary, if I were to describe her in one word it would be warmth. Like Terry, when you talk to Mary you get the feeling of a warm, loving, and caring person. She's energetic, yet peaceful, and she's softspoken and humble, yet strong.

Mary initially met Terry while in search of a good meditation class. She heard of a woman who could teach meditation in one class instead of in a week or in a month. She had also heard this woman was a healer, which stirred her curiosity. The meditation class began with Terry teaching the class a prayer before each meditation. The prayer was "Let nothing come from without and stay within that is not Godlike." With this prayer chills went up and down Mary's spine. Something was striking a chord within her. The group held hands and sang a mantra, "God is love." Mary could feel an electrical charge throughout the group. She felt exhilarated. She began to feel an uncomfortable pressure in her chest and began to cry. They were not tears from pain, but of joy.

When leaving that night, Mary was given a hug by Terry, and heard something that sounded like an electrical crackle. She let go and then hugged Terry again, and heard the same electrical crackle. Mary asked if anyone else had heard what she had heard, but no one had.

Mary was excited about what she had experienced and asked for healings by Terry. Although Mary was excited about having a healing, she was also apprehensive. Nevertheless, she felt that this was something that she must experience. Mary cried through much of the first healing and Terry told her that she was releasing stress. Mary asked questions and Terry's answers made sense. Somehow Mary felt familiar with what she was experiencing.

Mary returned each week for another healing and would occasionally take Terry to dinner with her friends. During dinner, Mary reached over to Terry and asked her "Will you teach us how to heal?" Terry gave a moment of silence and seemed to be taken aback, and then replied, "I'll think about it." Mary felt terrible and felt that she had insulted Terry. She felt that maybe she shouldn't have said what she had. One week later, Terry told Mary that she had prayed about it, and received a sign that she should teach Mary.

Mary has spent Wednesdays with Terry for the past

four years. She repeatedly states that she cannot put into words what it is like to work with a master. She's amazed at how much Terry can teach in such a short period of time and so simply. Mary feels very humble to be working with a master. (My personal view of Terry is that she is someone who does not quote verses from the <u>Bible</u>, but lives the laws, commandments and teachings of the <u>Bible</u>.)

The first healing that Mary did by herself was on her daughter. Her daughter had been getting many earaches off and on for years. One night Mary came home and found her daughter in pain from an earache. She decided to try a healing. Mary began putting energy in and then did a "pull-out." This is where you pull out the negative energy associated with or causing the pain. Mary felt the pain enter her hand, and then she let it go. The earache went away. She remarked to herself, "This stuff really works." Mary was ecstatic.

Mary worked on a child with strabismus (see strabismus), and was partly responsible for his remarkable cure. During a healing on him, she felt tremendous energy pass through her to the child. After the healing, the child was unsteady in his walk. Later that night in meditation she felt the same burning energy that she had felt during the healing. It was like a red hot poker sticking through her arm. Within a month, the child's thick glasses were no longer needed.

One day, during meditation, Terry asked Mary why she didn't bend her legs properly. Mary stated that she had injured her knee several times while skiing, and had problems with her knee ever since. Terry put energy into her knee and then did a pull-out. Mary could hear the energy being put in and being pulled out. Within a month, she could bend her knee and has had no further problems.

Mary was also plagued by chronic back pain and diffuse aches and pains, which she attributed to her scoliosis. She would get out of bed in the morning with severe back pain and had difficulty moving until she had her morning hot shower. Three years after she began having healings, Mary felt healing in her back during a session with Terry. A few days later, around Christmas, Mary found that she could not move. She was so stiff and in such excruciating pain that she remained in bed for two days. She immediately called Terry for advice, healing energy and moral support. Mary couldn't even pick up her foot. It took her one week to recover and since then she has had no more back pain. She had to learn how to walk again, because she feels that one leg is now longer. She did not see doctors so I could not attain the medical charts before and after this healing. Her husband says he no longer sees the scoliosis she had before she was paralyzed in bed.

When Mary's daughter was born, she felt that something was not quite right. Two weeks after giving birth, Mary stood back and said "What is it with this child." She felt that something was wrong between them. When her child was old enough for kindergarten there was the usual separation anxiety when Mary left her daughter, but after a while this should have resolved. Instead there was a neurotic clinging to Mary by her child. She would't let go. As the year progressed the problem became worse, and her teachers all agreed that this was abnormal. However, nothing could be pinpointed at home as the cause of this abnormal behavior.

Mary took her daughter to Terry and after one healing the problem was cured. At the age of 5, Mary's daughter said I've got to thank Terry for helping us. Her daughter drew a picture of Terry with rays of light coming in through her head and rays of light coming out through her hands. Then she gave the picture to Terry as a gift. See Figure 17 page 80. (NOTE that Mary wrote Love, Jenny, as requested by her daughter.)

Mary feels that healing was what she was destined to do. She considers it her calling and healing is now a big part of her life. She continues to do healings with Terry every Wednesday. Mary has not started on her own yet. Although she's been given the gift, she feels she is not ready. She needs a boost of self-confidence. Don't wait too long Mary, the world and many sick people are waiting for your gift to help them.

CONCLUSION

It is my perception that many doctors have seen in their practices what I have seen and experienced. A certain amount of skepticism within the medical and scientific communities is good and necessary, however, I hope they will have open minds. Political debates will not determine the truthfulness of the healing power. What is needed is scientific research. Only by controlled studies and the scientific method will we prove or disprove the healing power.

Again I resolve, the most powerful tool we have in fighting disease is modern day medical technology combined with the healing power. My hope is that western medicine will come to understand and accept the healing power and its role in the health care system.

GLOSSARY

AMNIOCENTESIS- a surgical procedure, whereby a needle is passed into the uterus (womb) of a pregnant woman, and amniotic fluid that surrounds the fetus is removed. The amniotic fluid is then analyzed for genetic defects of the fetus (unborn child).

ANTI-INFLAMMATORY DRUGS- drugs used to minimize inflammation of tissues. These drugs are often used to treat arthritis.

ANXIETY ATTACK (PANIC ATTACK)- acute or sudden onset of severe anxiety.

ATOMIC THEORY- theory that all matter is composed of building blocks called atoms. This theory has been well substantiated by scientists.

AURA- see human energy field.

CAT SCAN- a picture of the inside of the human body produced by a machine that emits X-rays, which pass through the human body and are recorded and analyzed by a computer.

CATALYST- a substance that accelerates speed of a process. In chemistry a catalyst accelerates the speed of a chemical reaction.

CHAKRAS- energy centers in the human energy field. They are vortexes of whirling high vibrational energy, where high vibrational energy can leave or enter the human energy field.

CHEMOTHERAPY- treatment of cancer with drugs, which are usually highly toxic.

CORONARY ANGIOGRAM- a surgical procedure performed by heart doctors to confirm the diagnosis of coronary artery disease. Performed by inserting a long catheter through a vein in the leg and injecting dye in the heart.

DIAGNOSIS- indentifying a disease from patient's complaints and physical signs.

DNA - an extremely long molecule found in each cell of our body, which contains all the genetic information to make our body. This information is passed on from generation to generation via the sperm of the man and egg of the woman.

ELECTROMAGNETIC RADIATION- energy with electrical and magnetic properties. This includes ultra-violet light, visible light, infrared light, microwaves, radio waves, etc.

GYNECOLOGIST- a medical doctor who treats diseases of the genital tract in women.

HAMMER TOE- excessive angulation of a toe.

HEALING POWER- an invisible, universal force which creates positive changes in humans toward a state of health and well-being. Its purpose is life and it is the force behind miraculous cures.

HIGHER DIMENSIONS- in theory, a place outside of space and time, where the kingdom of heaven exists. The higher dimensions include the fourth and fifth dimensions. We live in the third dimension.

HIGH VIBRATIONAL ENERGY- energy that surrounds us, permeates us and makes up our human energy field. An energy of high vibrational frequency.

HIV TESTING- a test for the AIDS virus. If the test result is HIV positive then the person being tested has the AIDS virus. If the test result is HIV negative then the person being tested does not have the AIDS virus.

HUMAN ENERGY FIELD- an egg-shaped field of

high vibrational energy that surrounds our bodies, (see Figure 12 on page 75.) Many healers can see and feel this field, and it is commonly referred to as the human aura. It changes in color and radiation depending on the state of health of the body, emotions, mind and spirit.

IMMUNE SYSTEM- the part of our body that fights infection, foreign substances and cancer.

INFERTILITY- the inability of a man and a woman to conceive their own child.

INTERCOSTAL NEURALGIA- pain following the course of the intercostal nerve. *NOTE*- in Louise's case this condition produced pain in the area of her shoulder.

LAW OF PHYSICS- a proven ralationship or phenomenon. For example, physicists have proven the law of gravity and the law of conservation of energy. (Also see theory).

MASS- property of a body, material or energy that causes it to have inertia or gravitational pull.

MIND-BODY CONNECTION- a theory that the mind and the body influence the health of each other. For example, the body can be healed if you heal the mind. Furthermore, the belief that we all have the ability to heal ourselves.

MOONIES- a nickname used by some people to identify the members of a Christian church started in Korea by Reverend Moon. They use chants in this church, which are not typically used in Christian churches.

MONONUCLEOSIS- a disease caused by a virus, characterized by tiredness, fever, sore throat and swollen lymph nodes under the jaw.

MRI (MAGNETIC RESONANCE IMAGING)- a picture of the inside of the human body produced by putting the human body inside a powerful magnet.

ONCOLOGIST- a medical doctor who specializes in the treatment of cancer.

PELVIC PAIN- pain coming from the lower trunk of the body.

POWER SPOTS- Certain places on the earth, where high vibrational energy is concentrated. These are places where miracles are known to occur and some examples are Lourdes, France and Chimayo, New Mexico.

PROGNOSIS- probability of recovery anticipated from the usual course of the disease.

PROSTATE- a gland in men located beneath the bladder.

PSYCHONEUROIMMUNOLOGY- a specialized field of medicine dealing with the minds ability to effect our immune system and thereby effect our state of health.

QUANTUM LEAP- an abrupt transition from one level to another level. For example, an electron of an atom will not take gradually larger orbits around the nucleus when it takes on energy, instead it takes a quantum leap to the next energy level.

QUANTUM MECHANICS- a modality of mathematical probability, that allows scientists to explain observed behavior of electrons in atoms and molecules.

RHEUMATOID DISEASE- disease of joints, muscles, tendons and connective tissue characterized by inflammation, pain, stiffness and limited motion.

SCHIZOPHRENIA- a disease of the mind, which is characterized by disordered thinking, retreat from reality, hallucinations and delusions.

SHOCK TREATMENTS (ELECTROCONVULSIVE THERAPY)- electricity passing through the brain through electrodes placed on the sides of the head. This is used to treat depression and sometimes certain forms of schizophrenia.

STRESS TEST- a test used by heart doctors to screen for coronary artery disease.

SUBTLE ENERGIES- another term for high vibrational energy.

THEORY- a working model developed by scientists to help them understand an observed phenomenon. This is an unproven model as opposed to a law, which has been proven.

THEORY OF RELATIVITY- a theory developed by Einstein that states that time is not constant throughout the universe; time is relative to where you are in the universe. This theory has been substantiated by scientific experiments.

TUBERCULOSIS- an infection primarily of the lungs, which is highly contagious and can be very debilitating.

UROLOGIST- a medical doctor who specializes in the treatment of diseases of the urinary tract (kidneys, bladder) and the male genitals.

VERTEBRAE- the bones that make up the spine.

BIBLIOGRAPHY

The Bible; St John 1-9.

The Book of Mormon and Doctrine and Covenants; D & C 76-70 & 78; D & C 88-37; D & C 137- 7 & 8.

Peshel RE. Peshel ER.- Medical Miracles from a Physician Scientists Viewpoint. *Perspectives in Biology and Medicine.* 31(3):391-404, 1988 Spring.

Everson, T.C., and Cole, W.H. Spontaneous Regression of Cancer: Preliminary Report. *Annals of Surgery.* 144:366-379, 1956.

Everson, T.C. *Spontaneous Regression of Cancer.* Conn. Med. 22:637-643, 1958.

Everson, T.C. *Spontaneous Regression of Cancer.* Ann. N.Y. Acd. Sci. 114:721-735, 1964.

King DE, Sobal J. DeForge BR; Family Practice Patients' Experiences and Beliefs in Faith Healing. *Journal of Family Practice.* 27(5): 505-8, 1988 November.

Grad B. Cadoret R.J., Paul GI: An Unorthodox Method of Wound Healing in Mice. *Int. Journal Parapsychology,* 1961:3:5-24.

Grad B.: A Telekinetic Effect on Plant Growth. *Int. Journal Parapsychology,* 1963:5:117-133.

Grad B.: A Telekinetic Effect of Plant Growth II. *Int. Journal of Parapsychology,* 1964:6:473-485.

Smith MJ: Enzymes Are Activated by Laying-on of Hands. *Human Dimensions,* 1972:246-48.

Krippner S., Rubin D., *The Energies of Consciousness,* Published by Gordon and Breach, New York 1975.

Ritchie, George, and Elizabeth Sherrill. *Return From*

Tomorrow. Fleming H. Revell, 184 Central Ave., Old Tappan, N.J. 07675, 1981.

Byrd, Randolf, Positive Therapeutic Effects of Intercessory Prayer in a Coronary Care Unit Population. *Southern Medical Journal,* July 1988, Vol. 81. No. 7.

Mersmann C., Melehan T., Wiseman M., Wolff B., Malgady R. Effects of Therapeutic Touch on Post-operative Pain NIH Study. *Pain Journal 1990 Supplement.*

Quinn J., Therapeutic Touch as Energy Exchange: Testing the Theory. *Advances in Nursing Science,* Jan. 1984.

Keller E., Bzdek V., Effects of Thrapeutic Touch on Tension Headache Pain. *Nursing Research,* Mar/April 1986 Vol. 35, No.2.

Ford, Marolyn and Boykin, Phyllis, *These Blind Eyes Now See.* printed by Arcata Graphics Company.

Pickney, Deborah, Native Healers. *American Medical News,* January 26, 1990.

Vasse, P.: Experiences de germination de plants: Methode du Professeur J.B. Rhine de Duke. *Rev. Metapsychique, Nouvelle Series,* No, 12, 1950, pp. 223-225.

Loehr, Rev. Franklin: *The Power of Prayer on Plants.* Doubleday and Co., Garden City, N.Y., 1959. p. 43 and p. 70.

Attevelt, J.T.M. Statistische gegevens M.B.T. de paranormale geneewijze. Amsterdam: *Nederlands Federatie voor Paramormale en Natuurgeneeswijze,* 1981.

Haraldsson, E. & Olafsson, O. A survey of psychic healing in Iceland. *The Christian Parapsychologist,* 1980 3(8), 276-279.

Geddes, F. Healing training in the church. *Unpublished doctoral dissertation.* San Francisco Theological Seminary, 1981.

Leuret, F. Miracle and faith. *In Proceedings of four conferences of parapsychological studies.* New York: Parapsychology Foundation, 1957.

Barlow, D.H., Abel, G.C. & Blanchard, E.B. Gender identity change in a transexual: An exorcism. *Archives of Sexual Behavior,* 1977,6, 387-395.

Benor, D.J. An annotated bibliography of psychic healing. *An unpublished manuscript.* Albert Einstein Medical Center, 1982.

Grad, B. A Telekinetic Effect on Plant Growth. *International Journal of Parapsychology,* 1963, 5, 117-133. 1964, 6, 473-498.

Grad, B. The "laying on of hands": Implications for psychotherapy, gentling and placebo effect. *Journal of the American Society for Psychical Research,* 1967, 61 286-305.

Grad, B. Cadoret, R.J., & Paul, G.I. The influence of an unorthodox method of treatment on wound healing in mice. *International Journal of Parapsychology,* 1961, 3(2), 5-24.

Hickman, J.L. Plant Growth Experiments with Matthew Manning. In J. Mishlove (Ed.), *A month with Matthew Manning: Experiences and experiments in Northern California during May-June, 1977.* San Francisco: Washington Research Center, 1979.

Loehr, F. *The power of prayer on plants.* New York: Signet, 1959.

Miller, R.N. The positive effect of prayer on plants. *Psychic,* 1972, 3, 24-25.

Alaska Bound,
A Life of Travels and Adventures in the Far North

A Book by Mike Dixon

━━━━━━━━━━━━━━━━━━━━━━━━━━━━

Stories originally published in magazines and newspapers across the country describe life in the Alaska outback as the author experienced it for 20 years.

For more information on this forthcoming book write

Alaska Bound
P.O. Box 804
Douglas, Alaska 99824-0804

MIRACLES AND THE HEALING POWER

HOW TO ORDER MORE BOOKS

Send a check for $17.95 (postage, tax and handling included) payable to Todd Dixon to the address listed below. A cashier's check or money order will speed the return of the book.

Miracles and the Healing Power
P.O. Box 21665
Albuquerque, New Mexico 87111
or call
1-800-381-5454